Leadership
for
Strategic Change

Brian Wallace and **Dr Christopher Ridgeway** are partners in the ODL Consultancy Partnership in Eton, formed 20 years ago, which specialises in counselling senior management teams on business-related strategies for change, the creation and assessment of competencies needed for future leaders, and overall management development strategies. ODL's clients include leading multinationals and 'blue-chip' companies such as Shell International, the Allied Lyons Group, Reckitt and Colman, J P Morgan & Co, Sedgwick International, Unilever, British Sugar, Abbey National, BT and British Gas. Their earlier book on *Empowering Change* was published by the IPD in 1994.

Brian Wallace moved from internal into external consultancy. He worked for British Aerospace, ICI, and, finally, Shell Chemicals (as head of organisation and management development) before forming ODL. Over the last 20 years he has been involved in board-level consultancy advising on the formulation of strategies for change, and counselling MDs and director teams on the right philosophy and the role of leadership in such initiatives. He has spoken at business schools in the UK and USA on change leadership and across the IPD network on HR's role and influence.

Dr Christopher Ridgeway is a chartered occupational and counselling psychologist. Before moving into consultancy some 15 years ago he held senior international HR management positions with the Burton Group and Champion Inc. His distinctive business orientation is most unusual in a psychologist, and he can offer consultancy clients both ever-increasing insights into the dynamics of the individual, and analysis of the factors that maximise business performance. He was a founding director of the Harley Group, a regional director with Hay Management Consultants, and MD of Psyconsult, a subsidiary of Manpower. He is chairman of the National Association of Psychotherapists. He is an active researcher and a contributor of many challenging articles to British and European psychological and management journals.

The Institute of Personnel and Development is the leading publisher of books and reports for personnel and training professionals and students and for all those concerned with the effective management and development of people at work. For full details of all our titles please telephone the Publishing Department on 0181 263 3387.

Leadership
for
Strategic Change

Brian Wallace
and
Christopher Ridgeway

INSTITUTE OF PERSONNEL
AND DEVELOPMENT

Typeset by Photoprint, Torquay

Printed in Great Britain by
The Short Run Press, Exeter

British Library Cataloguing in Publication Data

A catalogue record for this book is available from the
British Library

ISBN 0–85292–613–8

The views expressed in this book are the authors' own, and
may not necessarily reflect those of the IPD.

INSTITUTE OF PERSONNEL
AND DEVELOPMENT

IPD House, Camp Road, London SW19 4UX
Tel.: 0181 971 9000 Fax: 0181 263 3333
Registered charity no. 1038333. A company limited by guarantee. Registered in
England no. 2931892.
Registered office as above.

Contents

 **Foreword**

As we approach the millennium, the business world is replete with programmes which can generically be called something like *Vision 2000*, all saying very similar things; all setting more or less the same objectives. At the same time we are also faced with a plethora of business fads, all suggesting that somewhere there is a solution to our problems. A 1993 survey of change management by consultants KPMG found that most of the 250 respondents were running four or more different types of cross-functional change programme. The Boston Consulting Group reported that many US companies had up to 15 process improvements under way at the same time. Perhaps, to paraphrase Parkinson's law, the number of change programmes expands to meet the number of available consultants. In the United States between 1982 and 1992 the number of consulting firms increased from 780 to 1593 (104 per cent), the number of consultants from 30,000 to 81,000 (170 per cent) and consulting revenue from $3.5 billion to $15.2 billion (334 per cent)!

The programmes and goals advocated by both *Vision 2000* type programmes and by the legions of consultants cover virtually every aspect of business activity, but they generally suffer from a number of similar weaknesses. In this foreword I will refer to just two.

First, they are rarely about achieving the paradigm shift, i.e. breaking out of the established way of thinking. By this I do not mean that it is not important to achieve dramatic improvements within an organisation, but that real success comes to those who change the rules of the game rather than to those who simply perform better within the rules determined by someone else. Most fundamental change programmes originate from a comparatively small number of innovative companies – Xerox, Honda, ABB, Motorola, 3M, and not more than a dozen others – they are picked up by some watchful consultants or academics and are turned into concepts, publicised, and, if they are lucky, the

world beats a path to their door. After a time, most of them fade
away. But the real benefits come to those who were in there first,
those who broke the mould rather than to those who followed
after. One of the key principles of marketing is that it is better to
be first than it is to be best, and the same applies to managerial
concepts, for by the time the rest have caught up the best will
have moved on.

The second weakness is that they are rarely concerned with
the qualities needed to lead change programmes. Indeed, most
speak of change *management* rather than change *leadership*.
There are only a very small number of genuinely strategic
leadership responsibilities and they are all very closely linked.
They are to determine the long-term direction of the organisation, to ensure that the organisation is continuously innovating,
to lead the change process and to ensure that everyone in the
organisation is committed to these goals.

Christopher Ridgeway and Brian Wallace set out to remedy
this second weakness. Their concern is with the qualities needed
to lead strategic change programmes and their argument is that
unless leaders are able to recognise what is needed *in themselves*
their effectiveness as change leaders will be that much less. But
if that is all they have to say it will be no more than an
interesting read. However, their aim is to present a series of
analytical techniques whereby readers can assess their own
styles and behaviour and by so doing enable them to grow and
develop as individuals so as to make them more effective leaders
of change.

This makes sense, for how often do we find that change
programmes fail not because there is anything intrinsically
wrong with the objective but because their execution is poor?
And how often is the execution poor because the supposed
change leader knows very little either about the change process
or about his or her own behaviour patterns? We tend to believe
that because we are convinced of the potential benefits of a
course of action everyone will be converted. This is rarely the
case.

What we can do is to improve our chances of success by understanding what has made a number of change programmes succeed and how the lessons can be applied to ourselves. Ridgeway and Wallace's case-studies are full of brilliant learning points, which they match to their concepts of personal styles. In reading their book and completing their exercises I began to understand better some aspects of my own behaviour – and had a lot of fun in the process. You, too, will learn and enjoy.

Professor Peter D Wickens OBE
Chairman, Organisation Development International (UK) Ltd
and former Director of Personnel and Information Systems,
Nissan Motor Manufacturing (UK) Ltd.

Acknowledgements

The following managers and directors gave their time to the book through their willingness to be interviewed about their change process(es) and then to edit our interpretation of their journey. We owe them a debt. We hope they have provided some insights for you.

Eve Beresford, Group Personnel Manager
Quicks Group plc
Deborah Burt, HR Development Manager
UK Paper Ltd
Trevor Clark, HR Manager
Reckitt & Colman Pharmaceuticals
Norman Finnigan, Operations Director/HR Director
Grattan plc
Peter Hessey, Director of HR Strategy
Lloyds-TSB Group plc
Colin Ions, HR Director
Courage Ltd
Phylis McKain, HR Manager
Smurfit Composites
John Refaussé, HR Director
Allied–Distillers
Julie Sutton, Training and Development Manager
Grattan plc
Nic Turner, Organisational Development Manager
Do-It-All

We also wish to thank publicly Jean Khatib of ODL for her painstaking work in typing, organising, and editing our book.

We dedicate this, our second book, to our wives Eleanor and Tina for their continuing support, encouragement, and patience.

1

▚ Introduction

Sir John Harvey-Jones has argued that the critical skill for the manager of the future will be the capacity to lead change; though it may be difficult to develop, it is vital that all managers strive to achieve an optimum level of skill in leading strategic change. We strongly support this claim. Yet our experience in working with managers has made us aware that, though the organisational environment is rapidly becoming more ambiguous, most people prefer to believe that their experiences can be planned. In order to cut through such complacency, we have adopted a somewhat provocative approach and written in a style that some may find difficult. Lest this prove to be offputting, we thought it would be useful to explain why we hold the views and write in the way we do.

It is our firm belief that if managers cannot develop alternative ways of identifying problems and generating solutions, their abilities as change leaders will be limited; explanations based on extrapolations from past frames of reference will not be as useful as new ones. Alternative paradigms are necessary, because the organisational environment is becoming more chaotic. Even the businesses you work in have little certainty of continuance. It is salutary to remember that since 1970 60 per cent of the Fortune 500 companies in the USA have ceased to exist; this is a particularly salutary thought for those who expect a continuation of past certainties.

Our objective is to facilitate managers' capacity to lead change successfully in this chaotic world. We use several methods to help. Readers will learn about themselves and their style by working their way through a series of self-assessment measures. They can compare how they lead change with how others have led, as they explore a series of case-studies. Their self-assessment and case exploration will be aided by the change leader model that we outlined in our previous IPD book, *Empowering Change*. We have adopted a presentational style which assumes that readers' frames of reference will be expanded if they consider explanations that have emerged from a wide variety of intellectual activity. We quote from poetry, philosophy, psychoanalysis, etc. We do not expect managers to become avid readers of literature or cosmology; we do expect managers to become more open to alternative possibilities for explaining their situation, its environment, difficulties and opportunities. We are not alone in this process. Many business schools are searching beyond management theories for explanations of business behaviour. Some leading management theorists have adopted chaos theory. Reading this book, which may at times appear somewhat eccentric (but for a chaotic world, necessarily so!), will help you realise that you need to develop an increasing openness to novel explanation, new information, and others' ideas, in order to survive and prosper in this rapidly changing economic environment.

We refer to the process of reading the book as a journey. We hope it is an adventurous one: a journey of discovery. Because we believe that each individual will follow their own path, it is difficult to provide a map for the journey. However, recognising that most readers will prefer to have an outline of where they can go, we have provided a plan. You should use the plan as a compass providing the general direction of where you want to go, but do not expect it to be a detailed map. If there is a map, it is the one you develop for yourself. The president of Sony, Akio Morita, said, 'The only way to predict the future is to invent it'. Our contention, and that of many leading business schools, is that individuals have to invent their own future.

So to the compass. The book has three parts. Part One is intended to stimulate you to think about yourself and your organisation in ways that you might not have previously considered. The self-exploration is intended to get you to explore further your own change leadership orientations and competencies using our model of change leadership. Part Two, the case-studies, is intended to give you some models of how other HR managers and directors have operated in their change environments and have led their changes, both personal and organisational. We chose a wide range of industrial and commercial sectors for our cases, so that you can find some insights that are helpful in your own, unique, change environment. We developed the case-studies from interviews with the HR manager/director so it is their journey that you read about. Part Three is our challenge to HR practitioners to change to ensure they meet the needs of the future organisational environment and so become the chosen leaders of strategic change.

We may be accused of exaggerating, but where we have taken an extreme position we have done so to seek to ensure that readers are fully aware of the gravity of the need for change. We hope the book stimulates anyone who reads it to change themselves and then become more able to lead change in their unique change circumstances.

> Would that life were like a shadow cast by a wall or a tree, but it is like the shadow of a bird in flight.

When we began writing we were mindful of the rapidity of the change on which we would be commenting. At times we felt like T S Eliot when he wrote:

> What is actual is actual for one time and only for one place.

We recognised that we were seeking to provide models for, and guidance to, HR executives who would be operating in an environment which was likely to be very dissimilar to the pilot of a ship who, in previous times, would be asked to give clear directions to the captain. Because the existing maps would be clear representations of the tides and the geography, the instruments used to calculate time, distance and location would be capable of accuracy. The current corporate environment might be best described as a ship seeking to navigate in a 'whiteout' where land, sea and sky are invisible, and where, additionally, the magnetic north keeps moving and the continental drift is such that over a short time islands can move many miles.

It might be described as a situation like that of the early pioneers crossing North America, who, setting out for San

Francisco, were pleased to work with the maxim that if they kept heading west they would at some time get to the coast. Therefore, their deviations to miss Indians (competitors?), floods (technological change?), mountains (the Stock Exchange analysis?), plague (loss of a major customer?) and drought (withdrawal of finance by banks?) do not disable.

The navigator is therefore likely to be someone who has the competency to operate successfully in an environment where ambiguity is the norm; where he or she cannot claim that they are certain of the destination and absolutely clear about the route. The need is to have the capacity to be the corporate visionary who is constantly motivated to search the environment for factors which will enhance or restrain achievements of the corporate strategy. They will, additionally, be able to recognise patterns in the abstract environment, to link information, identifying connections in discontinuous data. Perhaps they will be driven in a way suggested by Ramsay Clark:

> Turbulence is a life force. It's an opportunity. Let's love turbulence and use it for change.

The navigator is therefore likely to be satisfied by this highly ambiguous situation; indeed they will be likely to enjoy chaos. Additionally, they will be likely to have the personal characteristics that will enable them to survive. They will be emotionally resilient, able to continue to perform at a high level even when they receive significant setbacks and experience considerable failures. They will be able to withstand considerable pressure, from others and from the environmental circumstances. They are perhaps, as psychoanalyst Rollo May suggests, people who believe that:

> Anxiety is essential to the human condition. The confrontation with anxiety can relieve us from boredom, sharpen the sensitivity and assure the pressures of tension that is necessary to preserve human existence.

Whatever the underlying personality state, they are likely to be people who are energised by pressure, conflict, ambiguity and circumstances that others will experience as anxiety-provoking and potentially disabling. They are also likely to be constantly searching for new ideas. It is likely they will be seekers of new explanations. Perhaps they will see themselves in Oscar Wilde's description of himself:

> I played with an idea, and grew wilful; tossed it into the air and transformed it; let it escape and recaptured it; made it iridescent with fancy and winged it with paradox.

Generally they will be seeking to find new paradigms which might be capable of explaining the chaos in which they find themselves. Always willing to let go of their current explanations, they will seek to find that idea which might light their way for the next period of navigation. However, as Remy de Gourmont states:

> Very simple ideas lie within the reach only of complex minds.

That is, the searcher for new, even simple ideas, is likely to be successful only if they are intellectually more able than most and have the capacity to recognise the new and adopt it. They are likely to have the 'Autolycus Syndrome', to be 'snappers up of unconsidered trifles', like the lovable rogue in Shakespeare's *The Winter's Tale*. They will probably adopt the philosophy of Woodrow Wilson:

> I not only use all the brains I have, but all I can borrow.

They have the capacity that Edward de Bono described as being able to:

> Think sideways.

They are probably driven to cease focusing on the logical conclusion and to re-explore the possibility of alternative explanations. As Arthur Block suggests:

> A conclusion is the place where you got tired of thinking.

The Chinese have a saying:

> To be uncertain is uncomfortable, but to be certain is ridiculous.

We are beginning to describe the personal characteristics that will be required by the change leader in the next century. The reason for using the number and variety of quotations is to suggest the requirement to be open to the thoughts of poets, philosophers, politicians, other cultures, musicians, mathematicians and thinkers from all aspects and conceptual biases. Perhaps only those who are motivated to discover new explanations, who have the capacity to assimilate these different concepts, constraints and models, can identify how to use them to understand their experiences. To seek understanding is to search for explanations. For Edward de Bono this is something most of us can achieve.

> Many highly intelligent people are poor thinkers. Many people of average intelligence are skilled thinkers. The power of a car is separate from the way the car is driven.

Our task is to help provide some guidance on what is necessary to be an influencer and which situations require different influence styles.

We will seek to provide guidance on what the HR professional has to do to identify his or her development opportunities and to suggest the direction of that development in relation to given change situations. Our guidance will be in the form of:

- exercises designed for self-diagnosis of change leadership competencies. It should be noted that these are designed to give only a general indication of type. They are not provided as a means of understanding the inner drives of the respondent nor are they structured to produce a psychometrically correct profile. Those who require such a diagnosis should contact a chartered psychologist.
- case-studies from HR directors who have successfully navigated particular changes.

- change leadership models which will enable individuals to explore themselves, their situation or the future to identify their potential and the optimum opportunities for achieving it.

We will proceed by describing a model of organisational excellence and an outline of the HR manager as an influencer of excellence. Perhaps, like Mark Twain, you will set out with a philosophy that:

> Travel is fatal to prejudice, bigotry and narrow mindedness.

We believe our role is to provide new visions, approaches and models so that those on the journey can experience their own insights, thereby enhancing their capacity to lead the change rather than react to the changed circumstances. We wish all travellers success on the journey. Remember, although we may believe we can *plan* our learning, we will be most successful when we are constantly aware of the random factors that influence us; the most effective will be those who are sensitive to, and most rapidly responsive to, the unpredictable. Perhaps Ovid should guide us:

> Chance is always powerful. Let your hook always be cast in this pool; where you least expect it, there will be a fish!

However, we recognise that the old Chinese curse 'may you live in interesting times' has become a continuing reality. Our insights are based on our:

- experience as businessmen where we have had to operate with others whose paradigm of explanation is that of the economic man making rational decisions
- search for alternative ways of understanding organisational life which has been helped by the theories of psychology, psychoanalysis, and organisation theory

- development, through our own search for personal understanding facilitated by our work as counsellors and coaches of
  others, and the coaching, counselling and therapy we have
  received from fellow professionals.

On these bases we have been faced with the conscious and
unconscious influences that produce the rational and irrational
behaviours of the led and of leaders.

We hope this work will help the leaders of this potential
organisational chaos manage their way through the environmental dynamic ambiguity. It is designed to enable the HR
manager to develop via some of the conceptual discussions we
provide; or through the self-discovery questionnaires; or perhaps
through the case-studies. Our aim is to provide all those who
want to explore their own thinking about themselves and change
with some new vision or new way to influence, or a new method
of facilitating others.

We hope it will encourage a network of HR directors and
managers who are motivated to improve their effectiveness as
change leaders. We hope mutual research, discussion and support will improve all our capacities to lead change.

Part I

Change Leadership Concepts: Self-assessment and Development

2

▚ The Change Visionary Leader

Managing in a more ambiguous environment means that businesses that have leaders who are more able to stand above the fog and can envision the future will be more likely to succeed. The concept of the visionary has its roots in the work of those who would call themselves strategic consultants, and in the work of psychologists and psychoanalysts who have explored the motivation of business leaders.

Strategic consultants would probably describe vision in terms of the capacity of an individual to define the focus for future business development. That is, they would describe the visionary as someone who has the capacity to identify the change in products and markets that the business should adopt if it were to be able to out-perform the competition.

The focus of business could be described in the matrix shown in Figure 1.

Figure 1
Business focus matrix

		Products	
		Existing	New
Markets	Existing		
	New		

The visionary would be able to identify the change along each continuum that would enable the business to maximise its performance. They would probably be able to achieve this vision because they were capable of both a logical-analytic analysis of the available information and were also able to search for alternative perspectives. That is, they would be motivated and capable of being innovative.

The visionary would also be someone who was aware of, and who searched for, changes in their economic, technical and market environment. They would tend to be almost polymathic in their understanding of the features which were likely to be threats to, or opportunities for, the business.

At their extreme, the visionary would be someone who had a capacity that might be described as that of a helicopter. They would be able to identify obstacles to further progress or opportunities to proceed at a faster rate through the chaotic fog and into the ever-increasingly dynamic environment. Like the captain of a ship, they would be able to navigate through the uncertainty to reach the required goal (port).

The notion of the visionary leader as a strategic thinker would tend to suggest that vision can be taught. It would be reasonable to assume that strategic planning can be taught; it is a process and therefore can be defined and each part can no doubt be described to others who can practise it and presumably improve their skill at it. However, the capacity to perform a strategic planning task is determined by thinking power. The strategic thinker who has a higher capacity to assimilate more rapidly more data than others is likely to outperform them. And those who have the capacity to analyse data more rapidly and accurately are more likely to outperform others. A third differentiating thinking power characteristic is the capacity to innovate. Therefore, those who can generate more alternatives to strategic opportunities or problems, and those whose ideas are unusual, novel or perhaps unique may well have a strategic advantage.

Thinking power is therefore likely to be a differentiator in the capacity to be an effective strategic visionary. It might also be considered as only the *potential* for an advantage, as thinking power without the motivation to use it in a particular manner could remain a dormant force. Many psychologists and psychoanalysts who have studied leadership have recognised that without the drive to operationalise the capacity to lead, the potential leader will remain just that: potential.

Leaders exhibit the self-belief that they can stand above the chaos and identify the patterns and connections in the information that others may not be capable of. They generate ideas for alternative market and products. They are curious about alternative ideas and ways of explaining the ambiguous environment. They tolerate continuing ambiguity because they believe that they, and probably they alone, are able to understand it and navigate it.

The visionary leader is therefore likely to be someone who is driven to act in a visionary manner. To be effective, they also need the thinking power to enable them to assimilate and analyse ambiguous data successfully and to generate ideas to overcome the problems and enhance the opportunities. It would also be expected that the visionary leader would be someone who was consistently seeking alternative explanations of their environment. A seeker of new knowledge and understanding.

The following self-assessment exercise is intended to make you think about your visionary motivations and capacities. When you have completed the exercise, which should be considered as a guide and not a psychometrically valid and reliable measure or an exploration of your inner/unconscious self, suggestions for your development are provided.

Enjoy the exercise! If you want to explore your motives and/ or your capacities further you should contact a chartered occupational psychologist or a psychoanalytical-orientated chartered counselling or therapeutic psychologist who will be able to guide your explorations. After you have both completed and scored the questionnaire, read the next section, which explains how to interpret your score.

Self-assessment exercise

How do you rate as a change researcher?

> Nothing in the world can one imagine beforehand, not the
> least thing. Everything is made up of so many unique
> particulars that cannot be foreseen.
> Rainer Maria Rilke

The following statements are designed to evaluate your disposition towards acting as a change researcher.

Please complete the following statements and then score them and make your own interpretation. Allocate 10 points across each of the three statements.

eg (a) 3 (b) 4 (c) 3   would indicate a roughly equal allocation

(a) 10 (b) 0 (c) 0   would indicate complete agreement with (a) and total disagreement with (b) and (c).

1 When faced with uncertainty, I

(a) ask questions of others about the causes of the problem

(b) try to remember what I did the last time I faced a similar problem

(c) analyse the available data logically.

2 Chaos makes me feel a

(a) need to create order

(b) sense of excitement

(c) desire to discover a cause.

3 I tend to be someone whose long-term view of all business issues is usually

(a) above 10 years

(b) above 5 years

(c) above 1 year.

4 When I compare myself with other management colleagues I tend to be

(a) about average in my capacity to assimilate business data rapidly

(b) a little below average in my capacity to assimilate business data rapidly

(c) significantly above average in my capacity to assimilate business data rapidly.

5 In groups of managers I tend to be the one who

(a) spots the relations between disparate data

(b) spots the connections between the current issues and solutions to past problems

(c) seeks to find consensus.

6 When I am reviewing strategic issues I tend to be the one who

(a) recognises the limitations in the analysis

(b) identifies future problems

(c) is able to undertake detailed numerical analysis.

7 I would describe myself as someone who can

(a) generate novel ideas

(b) ensure analysis is undertaken in a logical objective manner

(c) analyse complex numeric information rapidly.

8 Typically I will

(a) rapidly become involved in detailed information

(b) focus on the most important issues

(c) stand above the here-and-now, and constantly seek to consider future consequences.

9 My relations with other managers will be to

(a) consider them as a source of ideas

(b) use them as providers of information to support my ideas

(c) utilise their analytic skills.

10 In the management team I am the

(a) innovator

(b) analyst

(c) expert.

11 My management colleagues will eventually consider me as the colleague who

(a) remains open to their ideas

(b) is able to think through their problem solutions critically

(c) provides a reliable source of high quality HR advice.

12 When I meet in a group with my colleagues I will normally be the one who can

(a) recognise the similarity between the current problem and past issues

(b) recognise the relationships between seemingly unconnected data

(c) identify how the proposed solutions might relate to current procedures and practices.

13 I would describe myself as

(a) someone who enjoys ambiguity and is motivated towards situations of uncertainty

(b) a realist who enjoys providing practical solutions to current problems

(c) a knowledgeable practitioner who can always give guidance on any question about an HR issue.

14 I most enjoy

(a) managing situations where I can improve the efficiency of a situation

(b) managing the turn-around of a business

(c) starting up a new business.

15 I would rate myself, when compared to other managers, as someone who can

(a) rapidly adapt to a new situation

(b) quickly find ways of reducing costs in a situation

(c) swiftly recognise how procedures and practices should be applied to a situation

Scoring

Allocate your points to the two columns:

		1 **Change visionary**	2 **Maintainer**
1		(a)	(b)
			(c)
2		(b)	(a)
			(c)
3		(a)	(b)
			(c)
4		(a)	(b)
			(c)
5		(a)	(b)
			(c)
6		(b)	(a)
			(c)
7		(a)	(b)
			(c)
8		(c)	(a)
			(b)
9		(a)	(b)
			(c)
10		(a)	(b)
			(c)
11		(a)	(b)
			(c)
12		(b)	(a)
			(c)

	1 Change visionary		2 Maintainer	
13	(a)		(b) (c)	
14	(b)		(a) (c)	
15	(a)		(b) (c)	
	Total		*Total*	

Interpretation

If you have scored over 80 as a change visionary, this suggests you are orientated to the future. You are probably someone who:

- enjoys ambiguity
- will always stand above the here-and-now
- will take a future view
- will perceive connections in unconnected data
- will have a longer time perspective than others
- will have the capacity to generate novel ideas
- will usually remain open to others' ideas.

If you want to improve your capacity as a change visionary you should consider improving your capacity to be creative. This would normally involve you in seeking to think outside your normal frame of reference. This might need to be developed by:

- changing your reading habits. Perhaps reading more widely, for example, cosmology, maths, philosophy, musicology, anthropology, poetry, history of art, psychoanalysis, theology etc. This may develop alternative paradigms which could be

used to explain the future ambiguity. It will probably also
develop an increased openness to others' ideas.

- enhancing your capacity to generate ideas. This will probably
  involve what de Bono called 'lateral thinking'. It is likely this
  could be developed by some of the many creative thinking
  courses and, for those whose learning style it suits, by reading
  some of the many books on developing creative thinking.
- attending lectures or seminars outside your professional practice. For example, it could be useful to go to lectures on
  science. Could the study of quantum physics help you understand the complete abstract data on the cultural influence on
  new business in a developing market place?
- spending time with those from other functions so that you can
  begin to perceive the organisational world from their perspective. Be someone who is excited by other functions'
  operations:
  - finance, IT, marketing, legal, sales, distribution etc.
  - ways of identifying problems
  - ways of generating solutions to problems
  - concepts and frames of reference
  - theories and models.

♟ The Influential Change Leader

The individual's capacity to influence others probably begins with the concept the person has of himself. One way of describing oneself is the concept of locus of control. Locus of control describes the way that an individual attributes responsibility for events that occur in his life. Individuals attribute responsibility to things within themselves and to things outside their control. Factors which might be considered to be within one's control include personal ability, personal drive, etc. Factors outside one's control could include fate, luck, and the influence of other powerful people. People who believe they have control over their destiny can be referred to as having internal locus of control. Those who believe that their outcomes are determined by factors extrinsic to themselves are described as having external locus of control.

The influencer will tend to be someone who exhibits a high level of assertiveness and who acts in a proactive manner. Kets de Vries (1995) would argue that the power to influence will probably be based on the 'legacy of a stage of development in which the child has learned the intricacies of control, of dominance, and deference'. The adult who has this controlling power will tend to understand how to control their own behaviour and that of others through their confidence to assert their views, and their self-sufficiency to act before others and be proactive. They are also likely to exert control through their capacity to use the processes and procedures of the organisation to force others to comply with their demands.

The influential manager will generally be someone who will be able to push or pull others towards their goals. They will tend to push by using an authoritative, or in crisis coercive, style. They will tend to pull through their understanding and use of the available rewards in business. For some, this might be considered manipulative; for others it would be regarded as legitimate instrumental management which uses feedback to produce acceptable behaviour that complies with the organisation's demands. The highest performing manager would, of course, be someone who could combine the capacity to envision with the capacity to influence.

The following inventories are provided for you to explore your influence. They should be regarded as rapid self-report overviews. It is not intended as a valid psychometric instrument, nor an exploration of your inner psychic dynamics – your unconscious. If the process causes you to want to explore further then contacting psychologists or analysts interested in leadership style and its roots would be the appropriate next step.

Power drives

This questionnaire is designed to explore your power drives. For each question, you should write in the box the score you feel best fits your view of yourself, ranging from 5 (= absolutely as I feel) to 1 (= I don't feel like this).

1 When faced with people who oppose my views, I

(a) tell them what the rules and regulations say
(b) inform them that, as the manager, my views
    will be accepted
(c) try to understand their position, then work with
    them to overcome the obstacle.

2 In groups, I tend to

(a) try to get others to work through issues themselves,
    then work with me on my concepts
(b) ensure others know that I have the critical
    information
(c) seek to make others aware that, as the most senior
    person, my experience prevails.

3 In negotiations, I

(a) listen to the other party, trying to empathise
    with their views, and then work with them
    to seek compromise

(b) ensure I have the critical information, then play
    my cards close to my chest

(c) make certain that I have open communications
    to the person at the highest level so I can always
    use their authority to influence the decision.

4 In problem-solving situations, I

(a) make sure everyone knows that I have the
    authority to review the decision

(b) suspend judgement until I have understood
    everyone's views, then I work with them
    on the analysis

(c) begin the meeting by outlining the solutions
    I have previously provided for similar problems.

5 I tend to communicate a decision by saying

(a) I feel we should agree this because I believe
    this is correct

(b) I believe we should agree because this fits with the
    current processes and procedures

(c) you should agree this because as a senior manager
    I consider it correct.

6 I seek to motivate others by

(a) trying to understand their needs and concerns

(b) explaining that because I understand the problems
    and factors relating to it, my process should be
    followed

(c) recommending that individuals follow my
    judgement because I have more authority than they.

7 My way of controlling others' performance is to

(a) inform them of either the rules/regulations or
their performance objectives

(b) explain that, as their manager, I have to account
for their performance

(c) seek to understand their motives, attitudes
and concerns.

Scoring

Transcribe your scores to the three columns.

	Expert power	Personal power	Position power
1	(a)	(b)	(c)
2	(a)	(b)	(c)
3	(a)	(b)	(c)
4	(a)	(b)	(c)
5	(a)	(b)	(c)
6	(a)	(b)	(c)
7	(a)	(b)	(c)
	Total	*Total*	*Total*

Scores should be allocated at 5 points for each agreement between your choice and the one allocated above.

A score of 30 or more in any column suggests that this is a high level of power for you. Any column where you score less than 20 suggests that you might not generally use this type of power. Having determined if you have mainly internal or external forms of control, and then determined if you are someone who uses expert, position and/or personal power, you should seek to determine if you are likely to be successful in influence throughout your role set.

Personal influence patterns

The following is designed to give you some indication of your influence patterns. Answer the questions by deciding how far you can influence any person or situation. Indicate your degree of influence by allocating between 0 and 10 points to each question.

1 The degree to which I influence my boss's decisions is

2 The degree to which I influence the board's strategy is

3 The degree to which I influence senior managers' judgement is

4 The degree to which I influence HR peers at my level is

5 The degree to which I influence significant business judgements of senior line managers is

6 The degree to which I influence HR staff who work for me is

7 My assessment of how far I influence senior management selection decisions is

8 My assessment of how far I influence senior management personal development decisions is

9 My assessment of how far I influence senior management's development decisions about their staff is

10 My assessment of how far I influence board-level decisions about their compensation is

11 My assessment of how far I influence board-level
decisions about their financial benefits is

12 My assessment of how far I influence senior
management employee relations decisions is

13 I would evaluate my ability to influence the
decisions of my HR colleagues as

14 I would evaluate my ability to influence the
decisions of my HR staff as

15 I would estimate my ability to change my boss's
decisions as

16 I would estimate my capacity to change the HR
decisions of senior line managers as

17 I would estimate my capacity to change the HR
decisions of my HR colleagues as

18 I would assess my ability to influence HR
decisions of line managers below senior level as

19 I would estimate my ability to change the HR
decisions of line managers below senior level as

Scoring

Influence on boss	Influence on board/ senior managers	Influence on senior managers (below senior level)	Influence on HR colleagues	Influence on HR staff
1	2	18	4	6
15	3	19	13	14
	5		17	
	7			
	8			
	9			
	10			
	11			
	12			
	16			

Interpretation

Where the average score for influence is above 5, it is likely that you consider you have significant influence. Where it is below 5, you probably need to consider if you need to develop your influence skills. They could lead you to reconsider your use of control or use of expert, position and/or personal power.

Figure 2 shows a typical HR role set that you might have to influence.

You should now consider how your power drives and your influence pattern affect your performance.

Figure 2
HR role set

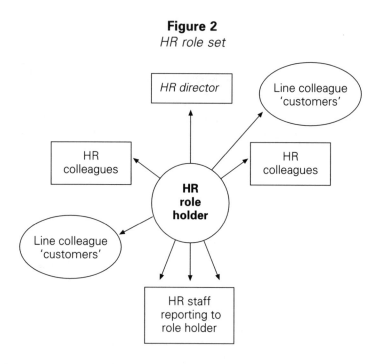

Internal–external control

This inventory contains 20 pairs of statements. In each pair, you may agree with one statement more than the other. *You have 5 points to distribute between the two statements in each pair, to indicate the extent to which you agree with each of the statements.* You may distribute the five points in any combination (0–5; 1–4; 2–3; 3–2; 4–1; 5–0). If you agree slightly more with statement 'a' than with 'b', then assign three points to 'a' and two points to 'b'. If you agree very much with 'a' and very little with 'b', assign four points to 'a' and one point to 'b'. If you agree completely with 'a' but do not agree at all with 'b', assign five points to 'a' and zero to 'b'.

You *may not* divide your points equally (ie 2.5) between the choices. You must choose one statement with which you agree more and then distribute the points.

1 (a) Competent people always will be recognised.

  (b) No matter how competent one is, it is almost
      impossible to get ahead in life without luck.

2 (a) Leaving things to chance and letting time
      take care of them helps a person to relax
      and enjoy life.
  (b) Working towards goals always turns out better
      than leaving things to chance.

3 (a) Organisational effectiveness can be achieved
      by employing competent and effective people.

  (b) No matter how competent the employees in a
      company are, if environmental conditions are
      not good the organisation will not be effective.

4 (a) It does not matter how hard a person works,
      he or she will achieve only what is destined.

  (b) One achieves one's rewards solely on the effort
      one makes.

5 (a) There are many events beyond our control.

  (b) People are the creators of their own life.

6 (a) People can determine their own destinies.

   (b) There is no point in spending time doings things to change one's destiny. What is going to happen, will.

7 (a) Even perceptive people falter quite often because the environment is chaotic.

   (b) When a manager's prediction of the environmental situation is wrong, that person can blame only himself/herself.

8 (a) These days, people must depend on the help and support of others.

   (b) It is possible to be successful without depending too much on others.

9 (a) Whether or not you will be successful depends on inherited factors.

   (b) People can become successful with effort and capability irrespective of their inherited characteristics.

10 (a) Some people can never be successful.

   (b) It is possible to develop management success ability in anyone.

11 (a) Whether or not you make a profit in business depends on luck.

  (b) Whether or not you make a profit in business depends on your capability.

12 (a) When purchasing goods, it is wise to collect as much information as possible from various sources and then to make a final choice.
  (b) There is no point in collecting a lot of information; in the long run, the more you pay, the better the product.

13 (a) Whether or not you get financial support depends on the bank manager you deal with.

  (b) Whether or not you get financial support depends on how good you are.

14 (a) People are often significantly influenced by things that they can neither understand nor control.
  (b) People can control events that affect their success.

15 (a) People fail because of their own lack of ability.

  (b) People are bound to fail at least half the time, because success or failure depends on a number of factors beyond their control.

16 (a) Whether or not a person can become successful
       depends on social and economic conditions.

   (b) People can always be successful, irrespective
       of social and economic circumstances.

17 (a) The best managers believe in planning their
       activities in advance.

   (b) There is no need for advance planning, because
       no matter how good one is, there always will
       be chance factors that influence success.

18 (a) Whether or not a salesperson will be able to
       sell his or her product depends on how effec-
       tive the other salespeople are.
   (b) No matter how good the other salespeople are,
       an effective salesperson always will be able to
       sell his or her own product

19 (a) Successful people are born, not created.

   (b) It is possible for people to learn to become
       more successful even if they do not begin that
       way.

20 (a) A person's capabilities may have very little
       to do with their success.

   (b) A capable person can always shape his or her
       own life.

Scoring

Transfer your point allocations from the inventory form on to this scoring-sheet:

Internal control	**External control**
20b _____	20a _____
19b _____	19a _____
18b _____	18a _____
17a _____	17b _____
16b _____	16a _____
15a _____	15b _____
14b _____	14a _____
13b _____	13a _____
12a _____	12b _____
11b _____	11a _____
10b _____	10a _____
9b _____	9a _____
8b _____	8a _____
7b _____	7a _____
6a _____	6b _____
5b _____	5a _____
4b _____	4a _____
3a _____	3b _____
2b _____	2a _____
1a _____	1b _____
Total internal	*Total external*

Determine the ratio of your internal/external control scores by dividing the total internal score by the total external score.

Record the ratio here.........................

Interpretation

Internal/external ratios above 3.0 indicate a high level of *internality*. Ratios below 1.0 indicate that the respondent has a more *external* locus-of-control orientation. The higher the ratio is above 1.0, the more internal you are.

You should now consider how your *power*, *influence* and *control* affect your performance.

If you wish to develop your capacity to influence, there is a wide range of development actions you should consider. Given that most influence involves communication, you should consider the degree to which you are able to structure your oral and written communications to ensure that they not only contain the required information in a form that the recipient can assimilate and understand, but that they motivate them to act in the manner you would wish.

You should ask yourself if you are sufficiently able to empathise with the recipient so that you can fully understand how they will receive the information and how they will act. You should consider how able you are to listen actively to their responses so that you can, if necessary, adjust your influence style to make it more likely that they will be convinced by your arguments.

You should ask yourself if you have the range of influence styles necessary to influence others within your organisation: upwards; to your peers; and to your subordinates. Are you able to influence upwards? Do you have the necessary awareness of those within the organisation who have to be influenced to achieve particular goals? Are you able to use *expert*, *position* and *personal* power and do you know when it is most effective and efficient to use them?

You should consider if you have the capacity to envision what the recipient will respond to positively and you should explore how far you are able to tailor your feelings, actions and words so that the maximum positive response is achieved.

Where you are operating in a multicultural environment, you should consider your capacity to flex your influence style so that you have the maximum positive impact on each individual, whatever their culture. A similar process should be undertaken if you are working in a global environment where you will need to be aware of the acceptable influence styles with customers,

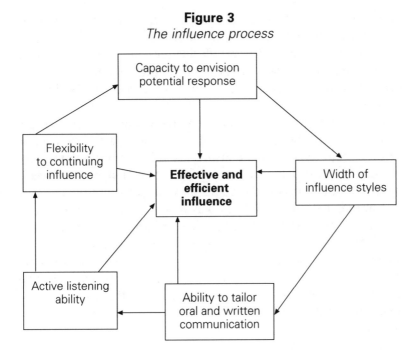

Figure 3
The influence process

colleagues and suppliers from other countries. Additionally, given that many organisations are becoming more matrix-based, you should reflect on your capacity to influence where situations are temporary or where you have little or no position power. The influence process might be graphically represented as in Figure 3.

The HR influence leader may act as leader of a project or as a project member. The project level could be strategic; for example, as a member of a team seeking to develop a strategy for globalisation. It could be tactical; for example, identifying members of a group who will be able to launch a new product in a new market. In all cases the HR manager can influence through his or her expert power: that is, they could in the new team area be providing advice on team types. They could be using position power, particularly if the team has HR members, or they could be using personal power. In the latter role it is likely that they might be seeking to influence via their capacity to act as process consultants, helping the group to maximise its effectiveness through their capacity to provide insights into such matters as: what each person appears to be contributing; members' influencing behaviour on each other; how people seem to be feeling, etc.

To become more influential, it is likely that the HR manager will have to develop change agent capacities. They will have to be more able to act in the consultancy role. To achieve this role change they will have to develop their knowledge of organisation, team and individual models, as well as having the capacity to communicate these models and relate them to 'bottom line' efforts and be able to facilitate others' ability to change.

HR manager influence is likely to be indirect, through others, rather than direct, although it does not preclude the need for them to be assertive and proactive influencers, who, because they are confident and feel they can challenge the *status quo*, are able independently to confront the accepted processes, practices and procedures.

4

The Facilitative Change Leader

Only the person who has faith in himself is able to be faithful to others.

Erich Fromm

The HR role developed in some ways out of the facilitator tradition. Some of the early personnel staff were primarily welfare-oriented. They were the helpers of those who had some problems in or out of work. That tradition was subordinated to the expert power positions occupied by the HR managers of the 1970s and 1980s whose roles were primarily determined by employment law, IR, or the compensation and benefits authorities. Although there remains a need for HR to have specialist knowledge of compensation and benefits and/or to be able to provide advice on IR, dismissals, etc, it is likely that this role has diminished and will probably continue to do so (some of the case-studies confirm this).

The future role of HR is likely to include a considerable need for the HR person to be able to facilitate others through change. To achieve this role, HR managers will need to have a level of self-adjustment that is above average. They will need to be energised by pressure; motivated by change and the need to adjust rapidly; and they will be highly resilient to personal criticism and setbacks. They will need a very high level of capacity to cope with stress, and they will have a deep understanding of their own motivations, feelings and attitudes and will fully understand how these influence others.

The HR manager who is to be a successful facilitator will be someone with whom others believe they can be open and who they trust. They will also be able to adjust their behaviour so that others feel they are fully engaged. It is likely they would have all the characteristics of an effective counsellor. Coaching and mentorship would also be competencies that the successful facilitator would have. Diagramatically, the capacity to facilitate would be represented as in Figure 4.

Figure 4

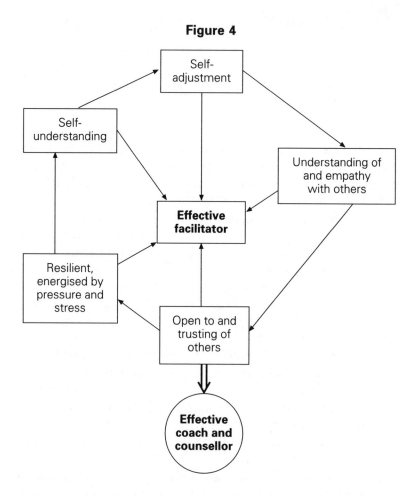

Change facilitator

The following questionnaire is designed to help you to understand how well you fit the profile of someone who is motivated to act as a change facilitator.

Allocate 10 points across each of the three statements.

eg (a) 3 (b) 3 (c) 4 would indicate a roughly equal agreement with each of the three statements

(a) 0 (b) 0 (c) 10 would indicate that you disagree with both (a) and (b) but agree totally with (c).

When you have completed the questionnaire, score and interpret it; then seek to determine what, if any, development opportunity exists and decide what development you wish to undertake.

1 (a) I know my own mind. ☐

(b) I always try to seek others' opinions. ☐

(c) Rapid action determines that I act independently. ☐

2 (a) I usually understand others' motives. ☐

(b) I am confident of my own views. ☐

(c) To achieve I have to be self-sufficient. ☐

3 (a) I seek to make sure I compete and win. ☐

(b) I normally work hard to understand others' concerns. ☐

(c) I recognise that I cannot be successful if I have to help others fulfil their desires. ☐

4 (a) I achieve more by empathising with those in my group. ☐

(b) I am successful because I compete against my own high standards. ☐

(c) My goals are achieved because I am tenacious. ☐

5 (a) I am always clear about my personal goals. ☐

(b) I internalise how others see the world. ☐

(c) I am sure I have the personal power to be the best. ☐

6 (a) My major group skill is that I can persuade
      others to accept my viewpoint.
  (b) I am normally the leader in any group.

  (c) In a group I always seek others' views and
      opinions.

7 (a) I enjoy helping others to develop.

  (b) I feel most satisfaction when my achievements
      are higher than everyone else's.
  (c) My highest level of satisfaction occurs when
      a group reaches consensus.

8 (a) I want to persuade others that my opinion
      is correct.
  (b) I want others to judge me as a personal winner.

  (c) Facilitating someone else to be able to reach
      their potential gives me a great sense of
      satisfaction.

9 (a) I am able to tolerate higher levels of pressure
      than others.
  (b) I enjoy working in a group more than on
      my own.
  (c) I motivate others by setting them clear targets,
      then giving them regular and frequent feedback
      on their achievements.

10 (a) I am constantly driven to try to understand
       why others act as they do.
   (b) My normal practice would be to assert
       my views rapidly.
   (c) I would normally be demotivated by not
       being personally successful.

11 (a) Personal success is the major driver of
       commercial achievement.

(b) Understanding others is the highest virtue. ☐

(c) I am at my best when I have a clear personal
goal that I can achieve in a self-sufficient manner. ☐

12 (a) Maintaining a high level of self-control is
something I can exhibit. ☐
(b) Seeing the world through others' eyes is a
major virtue. ☐
(c) Ensuring that others follow my opinions is
something I do well. ☐

13 (a) I am a very good independent achiever. ☐

(b) I am an excellent active listener. ☐

(c) I always stand above others' feelings to ensure
an objective analysis. ☐

14 (a) Others' feelings are the major factor in a
successful problem analysis. ☐
(b) Facts, objective if possible, are the main
determinant of successful decision-making. ☐
(c) I normally win because I can drive myself
and others to success. ☐

Scoring

Allocate your points to the two columns:

		1 Change facilitator	2 Self-centred
1	(b)		(a)
			(c)
2	(a)		(b)
			(c)

	1 **Change facilitator**	2 **Self-centred**
3	(b)	(a) (c)
4	(a)	(b) (c)
5	(b)	(a) (c)
6	(c)	(a) (b)
7	(a)	(b) (c)
8	(c)	(a) (b)
9	(a)	(b) (c)
10	(a)	(b) (c)
11	(b)	(a) (c)
12	(b)	(a) (c)
13	(b)	(a) (c)
14	(a)	(b) (c)
	Total	*Total*

> The go-betweens wear out a thousand sandals
> > Japanese proverb

Interpretation

If you have scored more than 75 as a change facilitator, you are probably someone who is disposed to want to understand others' points of view and to be able to empathise with their concerns, attitudes and motives. You also probably want to help others grow and develop and also you may well be able to be resilient to the pressures they put on you.

> The more you let yourself go, the less others let you go
> > Fredrick Wietzcke

To develop your capacity to become more able as a change facilitator you might consider developing your counselling skills. However, it would be reasonable to suggest that if you are not psychologically-minded, that is, are not highly motivated to understand others' feelings, concerns and attitudes, you would find it hard to develop and exhibit the required empathy. Developing counselling skills requires a deep understanding of at least one model of the person; for example Freudian, Jungian, Alderian, etc. It also requires that you explore your own motives, concerns, perceptions and developmental roots so that you can better understand others. This probably requires that you attend a programme where you have considerable experience of some form of personal counselling or therapy. Your skill in counselling is probably best developed by attending a course where you have to give and be given counselling and where you receive extensive feedback on your performance. Many of these programmes will be based on a counselling model such as that of Egan (1975).

Within these programmes it would be important to develop the competencies of:

- active listening, which requires that you develop your capacity to paraphrase what others have said; describe how others feel about what you or others or they themselves have said; ensure that the other person has had the opportunity to detail fully what they want to say; appear fully engaged in the conversation, that is, the body language has to be fully involved in what is being expressed

- providing feedback
- identifying blocks and enhancers to others' problems and concerns
- offering support and encouragement
- resolving conflicts.

It would also be important to develop the capacity to coach and mentor others. Helping others to improve their performance is about guiding and encouraging them to change and probably, as an HR manager, influencing their line manager and/or others to provide the necessary space and time for them to develop.

Acting as a coach will probably involve you in seeking to influence line managers to change their management style. It is difficult for an individual to develop when their line manager is authoritative or coercive, limiting their change in line with the direction of their line manager's permitted range.

By using your active listening competencies you should be able to help the individual or group to identify more clearly the factors that influence their problem and what has to change to overcome it. By asking questions you should be able to probe their understanding and their capacity fully to understand why they need to change and how the change might occur. Empathy will develop through your capacity to give feedback. This will require that they know what changes they have to make. It also requires that you are able to ensure exactly how they are progressing against the required changes, and what they need to do to continue their improvement.

The HR manager who is an effective coach will also be someone who has a high level of competency in their capacity to influence line managers to provide development opportunities. They will be able to convince line managers that developing the desire to learn, and identifying what individuals are motivated to learn, is a process which will enable the business to be more competitive because it facilitates the capacity of the organisation to adapt to change more rapidly. They will be able to encourage line managers to seek and provide development opportunities. They will also be able to persuade line managers that they and all their staff should be self-developers. Ultimately they should be able to persuade line managers that they should be role models who constantly strive to improve their current performance; are seekers after new learning; assess their own development needs; set their own development objectives; and evaluate their own progress.

For their own development, the HR manager has to be open to others' ideas and explanations. One of the qualities of the highest-level facilitation leader would be a faculty for constantly searching for new ways to explain organisational, team and individual behaviour. They would, when faced with an organisational issue, have a network of contacts from whom they would seek explanations. Generally this network would include other HR professionals, universities and business schools, consultants, professional institutes, etc. They would also be likely to set aside some time each week for a personal exploration of other theories, constructs, concepts and frames of reference. Typically, this would involve wide-ranging reading or other media programmes which would involve not only business literature, but also materials from other disciplines such as psychology, philosophy, anthropology, sociology – which are clearly related – and perhaps from some less obviously related areas such as theology, cosmology, mathematics etc.

To help others to change, the HR manager must be change-orientated. They have to be flexible and embrace a proactive philosophy that has at its core the acceptance that change is endemic and that successful organisations are those whose members feel they are encouraged and facilitated to change.

As change involves risk, it would be expected that the successful HR change facilitator would be a role exemplar of the change philosophy that only when the failure who learns is the hero are we a successful change organisation. This would fit with the example recently provided by Sir John Harvey-Jones, when he related that on meeting an American company's senior executives each one was introduced as being '. . ., our director of —, who failed to . . .'. Harvey-Jones was then told that each one, however great his error, had been publicised in the organisation as a hero because each had taken a risk and, though they had ultimately failed, they had learned through that failure.

5

Leading Change in a Crisis

Perhaps like Emmanuel Joseph Sieyès who, when asked what he did during the French Revolution, replied *J'ai vécu* ('I survived'), many managers who have sought to control rapid change would similarly like to say that they survived.

Achieving more than survival could be a major objective for the many HR managers who have to organise, plan and control a situation which is rapidly changing. However, they should be aware that logic and objectivity might not be sufficient. As George Bernard Shaw observed:

> Reformers have the idea that change can be achieved through brute sanity.

Or, as Alfred North Whitehead said:

> From the moment of birth we are immersed in action, and can only fitfully guide it by thought.

Or, as Edward de Bono observed:

> Removing the faults in a stage coach may produce a perfect stage coach, but it is unlikely to produce the first motor car.

As a guide to the manager in rapid crisis change, we suggest he might consider using methods other than a systematic problem-solving approach. He might try to understand the location(s) of the problem(s) and the possible solution(s) by other than a rational–critical thinking approach. Consider Goethe:

> Daring ideas are like chess-men moving forward. They may be beaten, but they might start a waiting game.

Managers will probably find that they frequently have to respond to a rapidly changing environment. This could be a change in the internal environment or it might be a change in the external environment. Internally, it may be that they have to respond to an instruction to change, in a relatively short time, some aspect of the technology, organisation structure or some management process or practice.

Many managers will have experienced a need to downsize rapidly. Whereas some years ago this might have been accomplished over an extended period, it is now typically achieved in a short period. Managers have to determine those who have to leave, and under what conditions, in a very short period of time.

Internal changes are frequently the result of a dramatic change in the external environment. Technological changes may require that significant organisation and process changes are made if a business is to maintain its competitive position. Typical of these changes would be the introduction of integrated IT systems which, if their effect is to produce performance improvements, require an associated process of business re-engineering.

Economic or market changes, such as the rapid decline of a brand because of the market entry of a newer, more efficient, cheaper or better designed competitor, may require rapid responses such as the acceleration of new product development or the acquisition of a business which has some competitive edge.

External and internal changes which are now likely to occur more frequently and more rapidly will require managers who are competent to lead the change. Managers will be needed who can lead dynamic change and whose competencies are those of the successful change leader; these competencies will generally be at the highest level. They will be able to envision possible changes and plan for them, better than most managers. They will be better able to generate unusual, perhaps novel, ways of overcoming problems; it is possible that others might consider them creative. They will undoubtedly, more than most, be able to review a large amount of complex and ambiguous data rapidly and recognise the connections and relationships within it and, therefore, be able to identify the key issues and thus rapidly be able to prioritise the problems and opportunities.

It is likely that their leadership style will include the capacity to direct others in a challenging, task-centred manner. The speed of change will make it difficult to maintain a facilitative approach; they will need to be able, where necessary, to adopt a more assertive, proactive, influencing style. Their approach to persuading others that they have identified a particular solution, or need to seize a specific opportunity, will be likely to include a more direct approach. This would tend to mean that their approach to communication and team leadership would be more directive and authoritative.

Personally, they would be likely to be leaders who enjoyed changing the existing ways of organising, planning, controlling and motivating; who found influencing their managers to be an invigorating challenge; and who were sufficiently outgoing to ensure that their ideas and solutions to problems were always visible to the decision-makers.

The successful change leader in a crisis is therefore likely to be a relatively independently-minded, self-sufficient, resilient manager who has a very high level of thinking power and whose leadership and influence style includes a high level of personal power.

The HR manager's capacity to influence and lead rapid change will be likely to be a result of their on-going capacity to exhibit an ability to provide strategic vision. If they have shown that they can provide added value to decisions on major business issues, such as acquisitions, mergers, disposals, major product launches, development of new markets etc, it will be likely that they will be included at the initial stage in discussion of the reaction to the significant external or internal opportunities or threats.

To achieve this level of influence, it is likely that the HR manager will have had to be identified as a business partner, not a manager who provides only HR initiatives. Some of the case-studies show how HR directors and managers have been able to change their role so that when a rapid change was required, they were included in the decision-making group.

Self-assessment exercise

The following questionnaire is designed to help you understand how you would typically behave during a situation of rapid change. Answer the questions by putting the three statements in rank order, eg:

I like soccer	2
I like rugby	1
I like snooker	3

In this case the respondent has indicated their preference for rugby, then soccer, and lastly snooker. You must rank all the statements. No box must be left empty.

1 (a) The thing that motivates me most is
      developing other people.

   (b) I am motivated most strongly by being able
      to conceive the long-term strategy.

   (c) The factor that will cause me to feel the
      highest level of motivation is being given a
      practical task that I can solve in a short time.

2 (a) I am likely to be most dissatisfied if I have
      to follow a procedure tenaciously over a long
      period of time.

   (b) I am likely to be most dissatisfied if I have
      to take rapid action with little thought for the
      future.

   (c) I tend to be most dissatisfied if I can't take
      the time to understand others.

3 (a) I tend to choose interests which demand that
      I rapidly take charge of others.

(b) I tend to choose leisure activities that involve considerable planning before I take action.

(c) I tend to choose hobbies where I don't have to take command of other people.

4 (a) I would describe myself as someone who is very concerned about trying to help others.

(b) I would describe myself as someone who is happiest when involved in abstract discussions.

(c) I would describe myself as being at my best when pushing or pulling others towards an agreement.

5 (a) Other people would probably describe me as 'action-man'.

(b) Other people would probably describe me as someone who excelled at conceptual analysis.

(c) Other people would probably describe me as someone who was at his best when helping others to maximise their potential.

6 (a) In my fantasies I am probably the leader of a cavalry charge.

(b) In my fantasies I am probably the scientist who by painstaking research discovers a new chemical compound.

(c) In my fantasies I am probably a counsellor helping those who were in a plane crash to overcome their traumas.

7 In a team dealing with the loss of a major customer I would be:

(a) the analyst reviewing the causes and seeking to identify the consequences

(b) the contact with all the possible replacement
    customers

(c) the process consultant helping the team
    understand the influences of their styles on
    the effectiveness of their interactions.

8 My self concept would be that I am

(a) reflective

(b) dynamic

(c) empathetic.

9 My team members would usually describe me as

(a) the planner-organiser

(b) the decision-taker

(c) the counsellor.

10 In a sports team I would normally be

(a) the goal-scorer

(b) the goal-maker

(c) the defender.

Scoring

Write the rank you gave each answer in the appropriate box,
then total each column.

	1 **Crisis manager**	**2** **Other type of manager**
1	(c)	(a) (b)
2	(a)	(b) (c)
3	(a)	(b) (c)
4	(c)	(a) (b)
5	(a)	(b) (c)
6	(a)	(b) (c)
7	(b)	(a) (c)
8	(b)	(a) (c)
9	(b)	(a) (c)
10	(a)	(b) (c)
	Total	*Total*

Interpretation

A score of 6 or more in the crisis management column suggests you may well be someone who considers themselves likely to take control rapidly in crisis situations. A score of less than 6 suggests that you would exhibit a style which is more likely to meet the needs of others. You might be a leader as described by Lao-tzu:

> To lead the people, walk behind them.

In a crisis, however, it is probably necessary to remember, as the Korean proverb says:

> Where there are no tigers, a wild cat is very self-important.

Change leader in a crisis – developing your competencies

In a crisis you will have to be more able to be a directing influencer. To develop this style of change leadership, you should consider developing your capacity to:

- confront underperformance
- be rapidly decisive
- be more able to give direct and straightforward feedback
- focus on behaviour that produces 'bottom line' performance and be more able to avoid discussions of feelings
- be more forceful
- be more proactive and assertive
- specify, in a clear and straightforward manner, goals and acceptable behaviours
- be able personally to link medium- and long-term goals to current tactics and be able to communicate your understanding to staff successfully
- delegate the short-term, tactical responses, and retain the more strategic overview as your responsibility
- lead others via your position power.

6

♟♜ **Leading Change in a Developmental–Participative Way**

The change leaders who adopt a developmental–participative style will generally seek to establish a trusting and open relationship with staff. They will have a belief system which places a high value on the capacity of staff to improve decision-making when they are involved. They will also believe that where staff participate in problem-identification, solution-generation and decision-making, they will be more committed to the implementation of the decision. The democratic change leader will generally be someone who will rarely give negative feedback but will tend to seek to reward involvement and will encourage teams to work towards consensus.

The participative style will tend to be successful when the staff involved are competent and when their motivations are met by the requirement of their role. Generally, the participative style will be effective where the staff are expert in their roles and the leader needs their expertise to identify issues and solve problems.

It will be less effective where there is a need for rapid decisions. In a crisis, it would generally be difficult to provide the time for total participation and consensus. Where staff have not developed to become totally competent, or where their fit to the role does not make them motivated to be committed, then a participative style would be unlikely to be successful.

Where a change leader adopts a participative style, it would be a natural adjunct for them also to exhibit a developmental style. The process of encouraging contributions and seeking to increase the staff's motivation to identify and seize opportunities will generally require a leader who also is driven to encourage staff to develop.

In a developmental leader style, the manager will usually be seeking to encourage staff to set their own goals, identify solutions to problems rather than refer problems to the manager, and constantly seek to develop themselves by looking for and using learning opportunities. The development style is likely to be successful where staff are motivated by the opportunity to self-develop. It will be difficult to act as development style change leader if staff are anxious because of some real or imagined threat, or are limited by their lack of capacity to learn or develop new skills or personal competencies because of limited thinking power or other abilities.

Development styles do not seem to be effective in crises.

Self-assessment exercise

The following questionnaire is designed to help you understand the degree to which you are likely to exhibit a developmental–participative change leadership style. You should answer the questions by ticking the point along the scale that you consider best represents your self-assessment, eg:

I like black cars.      I like yellow cars.

This indicates you like black cars more than yellow ones.

I like jam sponge.      I like ginger cake.

This would indicate an equal liking of jam sponge and ginger cake.

1

I tend to be someone      I tend to be someone who
who focuses on tasks.   focuses on people.

2

I have to be the one whose opinion is selected.

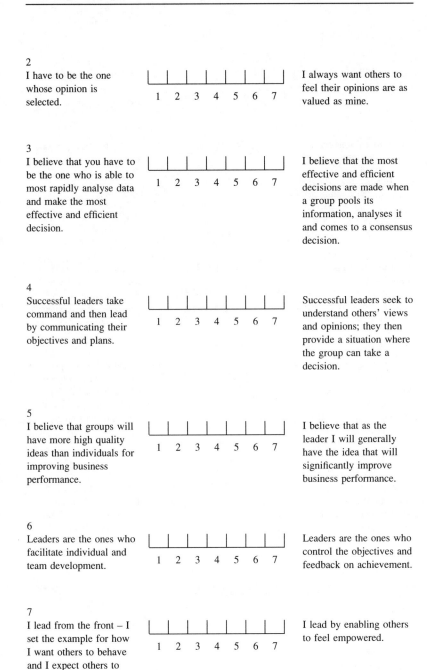

1 2 3 4 5 6 7

I always want others to feel their opinions are as valued as mine.

3

I believe that you have to be the one who is able to most rapidly analyse data and make the most effective and efficient decision.

1 2 3 4 5 6 7

I believe that the most effective and efficient decisions are made when a group pools its information, analyses it and comes to a consensus decision.

4

Successful leaders take command and then lead by communicating their objectives and plans.

1 2 3 4 5 6 7

Successful leaders seek to understand others' views and opinions; they then provide a situation where the group can take a decision.

5

I believe that groups will have more high quality ideas than individuals for improving business performance.

1 2 3 4 5 6 7

I believe that as the leader I will generally have the idea that will significantly improve business performance.

6

Leaders are the ones who facilitate individual and team development.

1 2 3 4 5 6 7

Leaders are the ones who control the objectives and feedback on achievement.

7

I lead from the front – I set the example for how I want others to behave and I expect others to follow my pace.

1 2 3 4 5 6 7

I lead by enabling others to feel empowered.

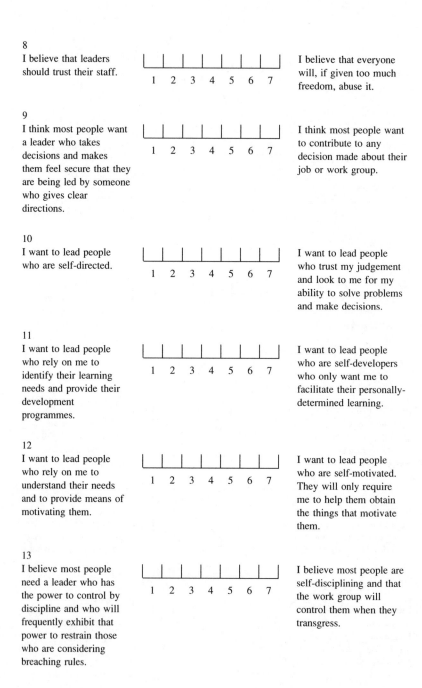

8

I believe that leaders should trust their staff.

1   2   3   4   5   6   7

I believe that everyone will, if given too much freedom, abuse it.

9

I think most people want a leader who takes decisions and makes them feel secure that they are being led by someone who gives clear directions.

1   2   3   4   5   6   7

I think most people want to contribute to any decision made about their job or work group.

10

I want to lead people who are self-directed.

1   2   3   4   5   6   7

I want to lead people who trust my judgement and look to me for my ability to solve problems and make decisions.

11

I want to lead people who rely on me to identify their learning needs and provide their development programmes.

1   2   3   4   5   6   7

I want to lead people who are self-developers who only want me to facilitate their personally-determined learning.

12

I want to lead people who rely on me to understand their needs and to provide means of motivating them.

1   2   3   4   5   6   7

I want to lead people who are self-motivated. They will only require me to help them obtain the things that motivate them.

13

I believe most people need a leader who has the power to control by discipline and who will frequently exhibit that power to restrain those who are considering breaching rules.

1   2   3   4   5   6   7

I believe most people are self-disciplining and that the work group will control them when they transgress.

Scoring

Write down the scores under the appropriate columns (eg, 3 = 5 means that if you ticked position 3 then your score is 5). Add up the scores under each column.

Developmental–participative management		**Authoritative management**	
	Score		**Score**
1 7 = 7		3 = 5	
6 = 6		2 = 6	
5 = 5		1 = 7	
4 = 0	_____		_____
2 5 = 5		1 = 7	
6 = 6		2 = 6	
7 = 7		3 = 5	
	_____	4 = 0	_____
3 7 = 7		1 = 7	
6 = 6		2 = 6	
5 = 5		3 = 5	
4 = 0	_____		_____
4 5 = 5		1 = 7	
6 = 6		2 = 6	
7 = 7		3 = 5	
	_____	4 = 0	_____
5 7 = 7		1 = 7	
6 = 6		2 = 6	
5 = 5		3 = 5	
4 = 0	_____		_____
6 7 = 7		1 = 7	
6 = 6		2 = 6	
5 = 5		3 = 5	
4 = 0	_____		_____

7	5 = 5		1 = 7		
	6 = 6		2 = 6		
	7 = 7		3 = 5		
		_____	4 = 0		_____
8	7 = 7		1 = 7		
	6 = 6		2 = 6		
	5 = 5		3 = 5		
	4 = 0	_____			_____
9	5 = 5		1 = 7		
	6 = 6		2 = 6		
	7 = 7		3 = 5		
		_____	4 = 0		_____
10	7 = 7		1 = 7		
	6 = 6		2 = 6		
	5 = 5		3 = 5		
	4 = 0	_____			_____
11	7 = 7		1 = 7		
	6 = 6		2 = 6		
	5 = 5		3 = 5		
	4 = 0	_____			_____
12	5 = 5		1 = 7		
	6 = 6		2 = 6		
	7 = 7		3 = 5		
		_____	4 = 0		_____
13	5 = 5		1 = 7		
	6 = 6		2 = 6		
	7 = 7		3 = 5		
		_____	4 = 0		_____
	Total	_____	*Total*		_____

Interpretation

A score of 78+ in the developmental–participative column suggests that you tend to believe and act as a leader who is more likely to be more people-centred than task-centred; more likely to believe in self-motivation and facilitate participative decisions. If you scored under 60 in this column you might wish to develop this style. The following are development suggestions:

> Integrity simply means a willingness not to violate one's identity.
>
> Erich Fromm

> There is nothing noble about being superior to some other men. The true nobility is in being superior to your previous self.
>
> Hindu proverb

If you wish to develop your participative style, you should improve your capacity to:

- let others identify problems and bring you the solutions, rather than encouraging staff to bring you the problems for you to generate the solutions and instruct them how to solve them
- encourage staff to set agendas for meetings
- encourage all staff, including the reticent, to participate fully
- listen actively to staff's ideas and concerns
- avoid your pre-emptive actions by seeking to encourage staff to take their own decisions by sharing their problems and solutions with their work colleagues
- develop your group process skills so that staff feel rewarded for their contribution and committed to consensus decisions
- encourage staff to self-develop
- personally seek opportunities for staff to experience career challenges
- develop your coaching and counselling skills.

Leading Change Where the Organisation Needs New Vision

The dynamics of a changing business environment require leaders who are able to stand above the here-and-now and can generate new visions for the business. The vision might be in terms of new markets, new products or services, or a consolidation of current products or services. It would include an analysis of the likely changes in the market place in terms of possible actions and/or reactions of the competition. It would include considerations of the likely changes in technology, politics or economics.

Leaders used to be able to provide a vision and then wait several years to determine if it had produced the required benefits. Current leaders do not have the luxury of such a delay; they need to be constantly surveying the environment for possible new opportunities and threats. The effect of 24-hour global trading and the real-time information highways means that the awareness of managers of what is happening in their businesses and the competition is significantly and critically increased. This means that the successful change visionary leader has to be, if they wish to add value, more able than the competition to spot opportunities and threats; to have a network of contacts which they can use to clarify or add to their knowledge; to give warnings about potential changes and provide advice and guidance on possible reactions to threats or opportunities.

Self-assessment of your preference for a new vision-type style

> Too often we forget that genius ... depends upon the data within its reach, that Archimedes could not have devised Edison's inventions.

We define genius as the capacity for productive reaction
against one's training.

Bernard Berenson

These two quotations might be the signposts to the change leader
as a visionary. He or she has to work within the factual evidence
but also to be able to apply frames of reference that are new
ways of exploring the evidence. The successful change leader as
a change visionary probably needs to be open to new ideas and
new information, entranced by new concepts.

As Alfred North Whitehead expressed it:

Ideas won't keep: something must be done about them.

The successful change visionary must not only be able to
visualise the new, he or she must be able to make it visible.
Within this process of conceiving the new and making it visible
to others, we need to be aware that what is posited is only a
position in time. Dynamic change makes prediction only a
subjective probability. As we have already said:

To be uncertain is to be uncomfortable, but to be certain is
to be ridiculous.

Chinese proverb

The following exercise is designed to help you identify your
style in relation to the characteristics associated with successful
leadership within a situation where a new vision is a major
determinant of high organisational performance.

To complete the questionnaire, tick the relevant box on the
range scales then transfer your score onto the 'spider's web'.
Ask your colleagues to score you against the scales and, if it
meets your particular organisational culture, ask your staff and/
or manager to score you. To obtain the ratings of others, copy
the questionnaire entitled 'Colleagues' and give it to the relevant
member(s) of staff.

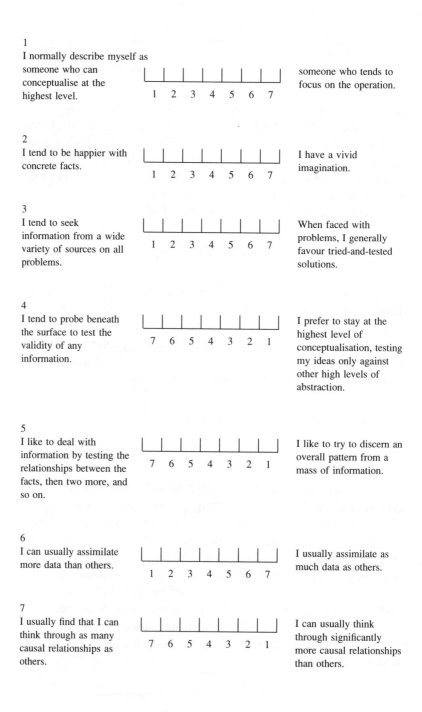

1

I normally describe myself as someone who can conceptualise at the highest level.

1 2 3 4 5 6 7

someone who tends to focus on the operation.

2

I tend to be happier with concrete facts.

1 2 3 4 5 6 7

I have a vivid imagination.

3

I tend to seek information from a wide variety of sources on all problems.

1 2 3 4 5 6 7

When faced with problems, I generally favour tried-and-tested solutions.

4

I tend to probe beneath the surface to test the validity of any information.

7 6 5 4 3 2 1

I prefer to stay at the highest level of conceptualisation, testing my ideas only against other high levels of abstraction.

5

I like to deal with information by testing the relationships between the facts, then two more, and so on.

7 6 5 4 3 2 1

I like to try to discern an overall pattern from a mass of information.

6

I can usually assimilate more data than others.

1 2 3 4 5 6 7

I usually assimilate as much data as others.

7

I usually find that I can think through as many causal relationships as others.

7 6 5 4 3 2 1

I can usually think through significantly more causal relationships than others.

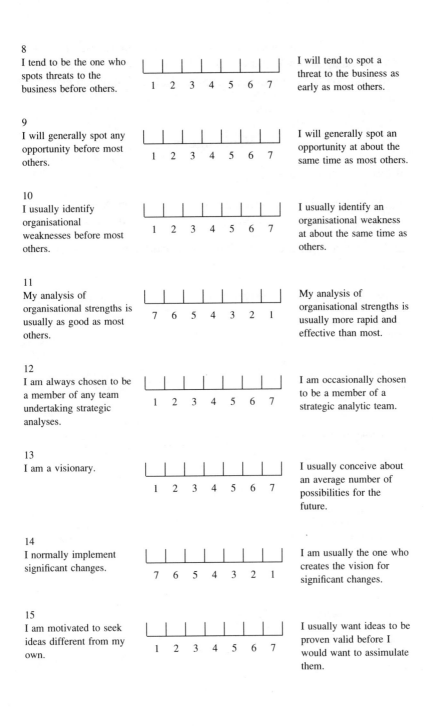

8
I tend to be the one who spots threats to the business before others.

1 2 3 4 5 6 7

I will tend to spot a threat to the business as early as most others.

9
I will generally spot any opportunity before most others.

1 2 3 4 5 6 7

I will generally spot an opportunity at about the same time as most others.

10
I usually identify organisational weaknesses before most others.

1 2 3 4 5 6 7

I usually identify an organisational weakness at about the same time as others.

11
My analysis of organisational strengths is usually as good as most others.

7 6 5 4 3 2 1

My analysis of organisational strengths is usually more rapid and effective than most.

12
I am always chosen to be a member of any team undertaking strategic analyses.

1 2 3 4 5 6 7

I am occasionally chosen to be a member of a strategic analytic team.

13
I am a visionary.

1 2 3 4 5 6 7

I usually conceive about an average number of possibilities for the future.

14
I normally implement significant changes.

7 6 5 4 3 2 1

I am usually the one who creates the vision for significant changes.

15
I am motivated to seek ideas different from my own.

1 2 3 4 5 6 7

I usually want ideas to be proven valid before I would want to assimilate them.

Give the following questionnaire to your colleagues, staff, and manager, and then ask them to complete it anonymously and return it to you, or to a nominated confidential and independent third party.

Colleagues

Name of subject: (Write in your name)

Status of subject: • Colleague   • Manager
(Delete as applicable)   • Staff   • Other

Tick the point on the scale that you consider best represents the subject.

1

He/she would normally describe him/herself as someone who can conceptualise at the highest level.

     1   2   3   4   5   6   7

someone who tends to focus on the operation.

2

He/she tends to be happier with concrete facts.

     1   2   3   4   5   6   7

He/she has a vivid imagination.

3

He/she tends to seek information from a wide variety of sources on all problems.

     1   2   3   4   5   6   7

When faced with problems, he/she generally favours tried-and-tested solutions.

4

He/she tends to probe beneath the surface to test the validity of any information.

     7   6   5   4   3   2   1

He/she prefers to stay at the highest level of conceptualisation, testing his/her ideas only against other high levels of abstraction.

5

He/she likes to deal with information by testing the relationships between the facts, then two more, and so on.

     7   6   5   4   3   2   1

He/she likes to try to discern an overall pattern from a mass of information.

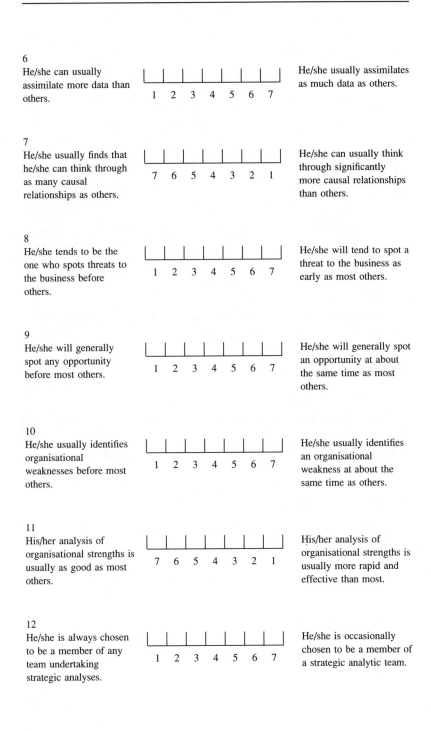

6
He/she can usually assimilate more data than others.

1 2 3 4 5 6 7

He/she usually assimilates as much data as others.

7
He/she usually finds that he/she can think through as many causal relationships as others.

7 6 5 4 3 2 1

He/she can usually think through significantly more causal relationships than others.

8
He/she tends to be the one who spots threats to the business before others.

1 2 3 4 5 6 7

He/she will tend to spot a threat to the business as early as most others.

9
He/she will generally spot any opportunity before most others.

1 2 3 4 5 6 7

He/she will generally spot an opportunity at about the same time as most others.

10
He/she usually identifies organisational weaknesses before most others.

1 2 3 4 5 6 7

He/she usually identifies an organisational weakness at about the same time as others.

11
His/her analysis of organisational strengths is usually as good as most others.

7 6 5 4 3 2 1

His/her analysis of organisational strengths is usually more rapid and effective than most.

12
He/she is always chosen to be a member of any team undertaking strategic analyses.

1 2 3 4 5 6 7

He/she is occasionally chosen to be a member of a strategic analytic team.

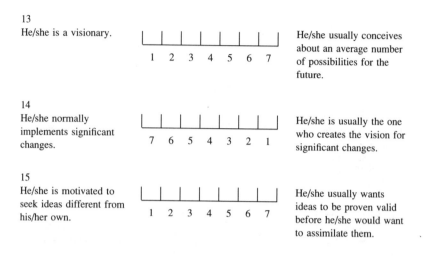

13
He/she is a visionary.

     1   2   3   4   5   6   7

He/she usually conceives about an average number of possibilities for the future.

14
He/she normally implements significant changes.

     7   6   5   4   3   2   1

He/she is usually the one who creates the vision for significant changes.

15
He/she is motivated to seek ideas different from his/her own.

     1   2   3   4   5   6   7

He/she usually wants ideas to be proven valid before he/she would want to assimilate them.

At the end of the questionnaire, add: 'Please return the Questionnaire to either the subject or his nominee.'

You should now transfer the scores onto the 'spider's web' (Figure 5).

(a) Plot your self-assessment.
(b) Combine the scores from your colleagues and plot their assessment.
(c) Combine the scores for your staff and plot their assessment.
(d) Plot your manager's scores.
(e) Plot any other assessments.

Use different coloured lines to join up the points on the web corresponding to each assessment questionnaire group (a to e).

Compare your self-report with that of your:

(a) colleagues
  • What are the differences?
  • Why do you think they have occurred?
  • How can you explain them?
  • What might you do to make them more positive?

Figure 5

Spider's web plot of your visionary competencies

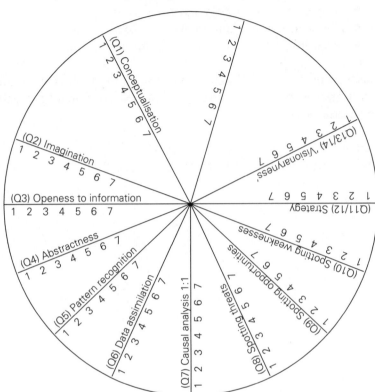

(b) staff
- What are the differences?
- Why do you think they have occurred?
- How can you explain them?
- What might you do to make them more positive?

(c) manager
- What are the differences?
- Why do you think they have occurred?
- How can you explain them?
- What might you do to make them more positive?

(d) others
   • What are the differences?
   • Why do you think they have occurred?
   • How can you explain them?
   • What might you do to make them more positive?

Finally, plot your 'ideal' against your self-report. Reviewing all the differences between yourself, colleagues, staff, manager, and others, ask yourself:

• what are my development needs?
• what do I intend to do to meet these needs?

♟ Leading Change in a Flexible Manner

Every new adjustment is a crisis of self-esteem.

Eric Hoffer

An assumption that people are motivated towards some stable state could be a justification for positing the proposition that the function of HR should be to seek to provide consistency in a sea of dynamic change. However, although this proposition might have some credibility, it probably does not account for the infinite variety of human reactions to the need for change.

GK Chesterton wrote that:

One may understand the cosmos, but never the ego, the self is more distant than any star.

This provides a clue to the problem of hypothesising a universal paradigm to explain human motivation.

The HR manager might therefore seek to lead change, conscious of the construct of individuality as infinitely variable. Some of those to be led will probably react to the particular change in the specific situation with dissatisfaction and potentially distress; others will experience the change as a positively motivating experience where they feel satisfied by the particular change.

The HR manager must consider the effect of change on his colleagues, his staff, other staff, etc. For each, he might ask: What self-projection does this particular person provide? What do I know of their likely reaction to a particular change? How do I believe it might influence their self respect? At all times, the HR manager needs to be aware of how little he probably knows of himself and how much less he probably knows of those whose reaction to change he is judging.

Given all the difficulties of knowing how one should react to achieve the highest level of organisation performance, it is probably not possible to provide definitive guidance on HR manager change leader behaviour. However, it is possible to suggest, given the previous comments about the variety of individual reactions to change, that an HR manager who can exhibit a flexible response to change will be more successful than someone who can offer only one style of change leadership. It is also reasonable to suggest that an HR manager who is more able to judge the particular change leadership style that will be most appropriate to a given change situation will be better able to generate higher organisational performance within the change situation. The HR manager who is more psychologically-minded (that is, more able to empathise with and internalise the motives, attitudes, and concerns of those involved) will be more likely to recognise the change leadership style that is likely to produce the most positive motivations toward the change.

The change leader cycle shown in Figure 6 is therefore one that HR managers involved in leading change should consider before, during and (for personal learning) after the particular change.

The following is designed to help you understand your capacity to identify the appropriate change leadership style and flex your style to that which is likely to produce the highest level of performance.

To identify your capacity to judge the appropriate style and to judge your style flexibility you should respond to the following by allocating *10 points* across the five statements. For example, the respondent to the following has indicated that he believes himself to be reasonably happy; reasonably thoughtful; slightly imaginative; not thin; and only a little anxious.

I am

Happy	4
Thoughtful	3
Imaginative	2
Thin	0
Anxious	1

Figure 6

The change leader cycle

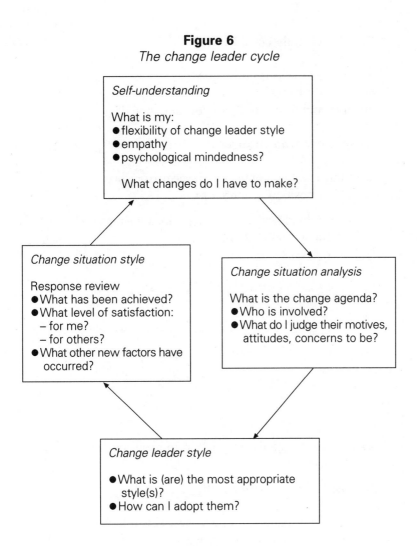

Please ensure that all the points allocated to each set of 5 statements add up to 10. When you have completed the questionnaire, use the scoring key and then make your own interpretation against the key provided.

1   Others generally consider me to be

    a) someone who is consistent

    b) able to adjust rapidly to new situations

    c) someone who understands others' views

    d) someone who commands respect from his
       or her position of authority

    e) able to hold strong views tenaciously against
       determined opposition.

10

2   I am

    a) able to change the way I lead to meet the needs
       of those led

    b) able to lead charismatically

    c) capable of maintaining my views even though
       others pressure me to change

    d) capable of adapting my leadership style to meet
       a wide variety of groups

    e) always a winner; I ensure my style wins no
       matter what those I lead need. They win with me.

10

3   Generally, I am the one who is able to

   a) think of a novel way to act to ensure I lead in
      the most innovative manner

   b) stick to my view to ensure the way I believe a
      problem should be solved is agreed

   c) out-run others

   d) ensure my expert view is the one with which
      others agree

   e) understand fully how others concerned with the
      change think.

10

4   My friends would consider me to be

   a) the one who takes command, gives directions
      and leads from the front

   b) the one who ensures how he or she leads meets
      the concerns and needs of all those led

   c) the one who sets the pace. Those who can
      respond as rapidly follow.

   d) someone who in groups finds it easy to adopt
      a variety of leader styles

   e) the one who has most of the novel ideas and
      who finds it easy to persuade others to change
      their ideas and adopt mine.

10

5   I generally consider myself to be

    a) an action-orientated person

    b) someone who can rapidly adapt to changing
       conditions

    c) a manager who leads from the front

    d) someone who can rapidly understand how others
       feel and then adopt a style which will motivate
       them

    e) someone who, given the choice between taking
       control and facilitating others' development, will
       choose coaching.

10

Allocate your scores to the following columns:

	Adaptable	Psychologically-minded	Wide range of change leadership styles
1	(b)	(c)	
2			(a)
			(d)
3	(a)	(e)	
4		(b)	(d)
5	(b)	(d)	
	Total	Total	Total

A score of over 15 in the Adaptable column would suggest you are someone who can adjust to changing conditions relatively easily. A score of over 20 in the Psychologically-minded column would suggest that you can understand the needs, concerns and attitudes of others relatively easily. A score of over 15 in the Wide range of change leader styles column would suggest that you are probably someone who has a relatively wide range of leader styles.

Developing your style flexibility

To meet a challenge in a situation requiring a different style, you will probably need a high level of coaching to make a significant change. Alternatively, if you have a high level of adaptability and have a wide range of styles, adding a new style would probably require only a short period of challenge in another change situation, and would perhaps demand only limited coaching. Those who have a low level of psychological-mindedness may well find it difficult to acquire a high level of facilitative leadership style. If they cannot empathise with a wide range of staff they may well have difficulty being able to understand how the staff feel about particular potential or actual changes.

9

▞ The HR Manager as a Strategic Change Influence Partner

Recent research suggests that there is little evidence that business has sought actively to explore the links between strategy and HR management: for example, Storey (1989, 1992). However, others such as Fombrun and Tichy (1984) provide American evidence that there is HR practice which is strategic. They show that in the United States there is strategic staffing, appraisal, reward systems and culture development, and that HR strategy can enhance innovation, quality of work, productivity and internationalisation. The contrast is interesting because it exhibits the difference between the USA, where there appears to be some conviction that HR is strategic, and the UK where the debate still continues.

Where HR managers recognise that their responsibilities and accountabilities can only be judged in terms of the influence they have on the strategic orientation there will be a high probability that they will be considered strategic. Where they recognise how their outputs will influence the achievement of strategy it is possible they will consider all their initiatives as possible enhancers of, or blocks to, corporate goals.

HR has operational responsibilities. It will generally be responsible for recruitment, reward systems, performance management and appraisal processes and development. If it can ensure that the test of each process or practice is the degree to which it enhances the achievement of a particular corporate goal, then it has a likelihood of becoming a strategic partner.

To achieve partner status, the manager has not only to be fully aware of the strategies but has to be perceived by his/her colleagues as being able to contribute to the achievement of the strategy. A model of the cycle of strategic influence would be as shown in Figure 7.

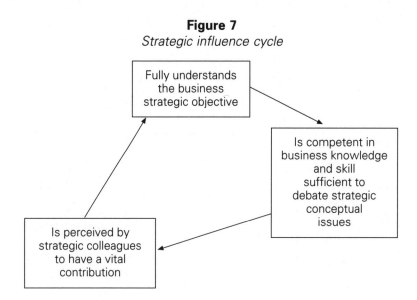

Figure 7
Strategic influence cycle

To be perceived as having a vital contribution, the HR manager will need to have exhibited a capacity to solve business problems. Diagramatically, this is shown in Figure 8.

The core competencies are the HR manager's confidence, independence and capacity to assimilate complex data rapidly and make efficient and effective business judgements. The HR manager needs to be at least as able as any other functional manager in his capacity to solve business problems.

Given that if HR managers can create an image of themselves as a successful business person – for example if they can spot a marketing opportunity in the same way that a marketeer might recommend a change in salary policy to ensure retention of 'high flying' marketeers, or they recognise a logistical problem in the same manner that a sales director might identify the need to change the competency profile of sales personnel from that of hard-line negotiators to that of business developers – they should be able to become valued members of business decision-making teams.

Figure 8
Problem-solving capacity

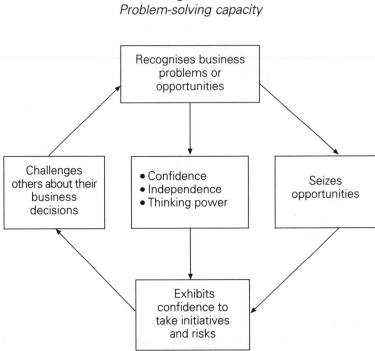

An HR manager as a business partner would be involved in the business's major decisions. They would, in the case of an acquisition, be involved in the decision to purchase rather than to grow organically. They would be involved in the choice of which company to purchase and the various legal and financial decisions that would result in the purchase.

These are the strategic processes in which HR managers or directors would be involved rather than the more operational processes that are more common; such as when, after the purchase, they analyse the fit between the salary and pension schemes or conduct HR audits to determine who will perform which job.

It would be expected that a business partner would have a similar role in

- new venturing
- research & development
- IT strategy
- finance management.

The HR manager would be a partner in the decisions about a company's possible joint ventures, such as who, in what areas, and how it would be organised. They would have a role similar to that of the financial director, who might advise on source and use of funds; they might advise on source and use of people.

They would, as a partner, advise on possible development projects. Not only as to who might staff them and how they might be organised, but what the appropriate culture and management style would be and, like all other general managers, how it would fit into the corporate strategy, and into the current finance, marketing, sales and production objectives.

Given that HR may be the major component in the success of any initiative, it would be expected that the HR partner would be a core contributor to all strategic decisions. Where Marketing propose changes in brand strategy or finance or IT in reporting systems, it would be expected that HR would recognise problems and/or opportunities and challenge on both HR grounds and on a general business basis.

Perhaps the best representation of how HR can be considered as a business strategic partner is where they are party to the overall corporate strategy and they identify the competencies needed for particular strategy developments and the associated business processes, practices and procedures, management styles and corporate culture. This is illustrated in Boxes 1 to 4. It is recommended that for each box the HR manager considers his or her particular circumstances and amends the matrix accordingly.

Box 1: *Strategic agenda*

Organic growth	New market development
New product development	Step out

Box 2: *Examples of required business competencies*

Organic growth	New market development
• Organisational efficiency • Tenacity • Methodical planning.	• Effective information analysis • Personal adaptability.
New product development	**Step out**
• Innovation • Initiative-taking • Proactivity.	• Confidence • Independence • Challenge to *status quo*.

Box 3: *Examples of business processes, practices and procedures*

Organic growth	New market development
• Efficient planning and organisation • Effective control systems.	• Two-way communications • Rapid decision-making • Self-directed learning
New product development	**Step out**
• Well-developed idea analysis systems • Reward for innovation.	• Organic organisation • Temporary teams • Empowered staff • Psychological contracts.

Box 4: *Management style and corporate culture*

Organic growth	New market development
• Authoritative management • Expert power • Quality-orientation.	• Personal power • Participative management • Open culture.
New product development	Step out
• High level of trust • Democratic management • Challenging but supportive culture.	• Hands-off management • High risk-taking.

Therefore, if more HR managers are to become strategic partners, they have to:

• ensure they have, and others know they have, wide business knowledge which can contribute to all critical business decisions
• make their knowledge and their business problem-solving initiatives visible in a confident, positive and assertive manner
• train line managers to use HR processes such as recruitment and discipline
• ensure that any HR initiative enhances the broad business strategy.

Partnership requires trust in HR management by the line. They have to believe that HR will achieve some critical difference by their involvement in major decisions; line have to consider that HR can achieve. Perhaps, as Goethe says, to 'achieve all that is demanded of him he must regard himself as greater than he is'. They must have conviction in their assertions and the courage and assertiveness to proclaim it. As Samuel Johnson said, 'courage is a quality so necessary for maintaining virtue that it is always respected, even when it is associated with vice.'

They need to believe in the ethical value of what they do. If HR managers can believe that what they seek to achieve will enable some greater good to be arrived at, they may be sustained when their initiatives, ideas and innovations are blocked.

HR managers need to believe that they have a critical part to play in the search for significant added value to corporate success, and through it to societal harmony. Perhaps we all are striving for a partnership which provides more than W H Auden's vision

> Almost all of our relationships begin, and most of them continue, as forms of mutual exploitation, a mental or physical partner, to be terminated when one or both parties run out of goals.

The partnership of HR and line should be more than that of the economics of supply and demand: it should be based on a mutual understanding of the ethics and values of the other. HR has, it would seem, adopted the ethics and values of utilitarianism. It needs to be sure it can sell to line the values of humanity which it has as its ethical base. That is, unless it rejects the humanistic philosophy of Macgregor *et al.*

A personal competency audit – strategic change partner

The following questions are designed to enable you to determine what your development opportunities are in respect of your current competencies as a strategic change influence partner.

Competency	Self-rating against current role	Self-rating against future role
1 Ensuring manpower plans support the organisation's strategic plans	*Low* *High* 1 | 2 | 3 | 4 | 5 | 6 | 7	*Low* *High* 1 | 2 | 3 | 4 | 5 | 6 | 7

Competency	Self-rating against current role	Self-rating against future role

2 Influencing board strategy through manpower analysis

Low					High		Low					High	
1	2	3	4	5	6	7	1	2	3	4	5	6	7

3 Consultancy to the board on occupational:

(a) health and safety

Low					High		Low					High	
1	2	3	4	5	6	7	1	2	3	4	5	6	7

(b) discipline and grievance matters

Low					High		Low					High	
1	2	3	4	5	6	7	1	2	3	4	5	6	7

(c) employment law matters

Low					High		Low					High	
1	2	3	4	5	6	7	1	2	3	4	5	6	7

(d) employee relations matters

Low					High		Low					High	
1	2	3	4	5	6	7	1	2	3	4	5	6	7

4 Competency at board-level recruitment and selection

Low					High		Low					High	
1	2	3	4	5	6	7	1	2	3	4	5	6	7

5 Competency as a personal coach to board-level staff

Low					High		Low					High	
1	2	3	4	5	6	7	1	2	3	4	5	6	7

6 Career counselling competency to board-level staff

Low					High		Low					High	
1	2	3	4	5	6	7	1	2	3	4	5	6	7

7 Facilitator competency to board-level management teams

Low					High		Low					High	
1	2	3	4	5	6	7	1	2	3	4	5	6	7

Competency	*Self-rating against current role*							*Self-rating against future role*						
	Low						High	Low						High
8 Competency as an adviser to board(s) on senior executive and board-level compensation and benefits	1	2	3	4	5	6	7	1	2	3	4	5	6	7
9 Personal competency as a strategic analyst and planner	1	2	3	4	5	6	7	1	2	3	4	5	6	7
10 Competency as an HR strategic analyst and planner	1	2	3	4	5	6	7	1	2	3	4	5	6	7

11 So that my opinion on this area is sought by board members and senior executives, my personal understanding of the:

	Low						High	Low						High
(a) sales processes, practices and procedures	1	2	3	4	5	6	7	1	2	3	4	5	6	7
(b) marketing processes, practices and procedures	1	2	3	4	5	6	7	1	2	3	4	5	6	7
(c) finance processes, practices and procedures	1	2	3	4	5	6	7	1	2	3	4	5	6	7
(d) IT processes, practices and procedures	1	2	3	4	5	6	7	1	2	3	4	5	6	7
(e) operations processes, practices and procedures	1	2	3	4	5	6	7	1	2	3	4	5	6	7

My rating of myself as a

- strategic partner, that is someone who works with the most senior level of management to envision, design and implement corporate-level business plans, is

Low					High	
1	2	3	4	5	6	7

- strategic change leader, that is someone who at corporate level leads others through change, is

Low					High	
1	2	3	4	5	6	7

- strategic HR change leader, that is someone who leads his or her HR team through change, is

Low					High	
1	2	3	4	5	6	7

Intepretation

Where you have rated yourself at or below 3 on any self-rating, you should consider that to be a development opportunity.

If you rate yourself at or below 3 as a strategic partner, then it is likely that this will in part be replicated in your relatively low self-ratings on your competency audit.

If you have rated yourself at or below 3 as a strategic change
leader, this will probably have been related to the ratings you
gave yourself as a change researcher, influencer, facilitator and
flexible change leader. If this is the case, then they are all
development opportunities.

Your view of your competency in leading your own team
through change would also indicate a development opportunity.
If you have rated yourself at or below 3, then it would be
important to address this need as it is unlikely that senior
executives and the board will value a strategic partner who may
have some limitations as an HR change leader. Perhaps the
development opportunities should be guided by some of the
following:

> Whatever is good to know is difficult to learn
> > Greek proverb

> It is of interest to note that while some dolphins are
> reported to have learned English – up to fifty words used in
> correct context – no human being has been reported to have
> learned Dolphinese
> > Carl Sagan

> From error to error, one discovers the entire truth
> > Sigmund Freud

To develop yourself as a strategic partner you will probably need
to

- improve your understanding of, and skill in, other management disciplines. Completing the relevant modules of a
  distance-learned MBA would probably help, as would periods
  on projects where those areas of your knowledge-base weakness were a high-level requirement.
- change the expectations others have of your contribution. This
  would require you to become someone who contributed in
  unexpected ways to the identification of problems and opportunities; and to the generation of solutions and their implementation. Board colleagues might have their expectations
  changed if, for example, you began to make contributions to

such areas as a logistics debate or a discussion on brand marketing or on the possibilities of using derivatives to hedge against currency fluctuations. Your capacity to contribute may well depend both on the depth of your knowledge and on your confidence in making your ideas and information known at the opportune moment. If you are someone whose reading of the financial and business press and whose attendance at meetings and seminars on business subjects makes you feel confident that what you know and have to say is both relevant and potentially novel, then you are likely to be confident and become more rapidly visible and potentially strategically influential.

Part II

Change Leadership Strategies: Learning from Case History

10

♟ Introduction to the Case-studies

In Part I of the book we have sought to lead you through a journey of self-discovery; a journey which we believe will have allowed you to take stock and reconsider the impact you would wish and need to make to influence change planning, thinking and implementation, as you and your colleagues aim to shape the organisation of the future. Our emphasis so far has been on personal development: we now plan to move forward and allow you to learn from other HR professionals' experience. In the case-studies illustrated, neither our case providers nor we ourselves would claim that their change leadership journey has been completed. All that they, and we, would say is that shared learning and insights from striving to influence challenge leadership and dealing with both the successes and setbacks, was important to them and their colleagues. All would say that they have grown personally and feel more confident to face the next change leadership challenge.

For you to maximise your own learning, we would suggest that you try to put yourself in their shoes. To try to imagine how they would feel as they sought to determine the change influencing strategy that they chose.

In trying to empathise with case providers, the following questioning process might be useful to you.

Understanding the business context

What was the business need and rationale for change?
What value and importance was placed on people in planning change?
Was change enforced by outside pressures or was it part of a planned, systematic evolution?
Was the focus short-term or strategic?

Influencing the leadership style

What account was taken of the prevailing style of management?

In choosing the change intervention, was the focus to go with the
flow, to seek adaptation or to challenge and confront?

How ready were the leadership teams to challenge themselves?

Who was really leading the change process: HR or the line?

Assessing the track record in change

What emphasis was given to the importance of people in
change?

What new competencies and skills were required? How much
effort went into empowering and educating people?

How important was culture to successful change?

What was done to change perspectives, attitudes and behaviour?

Planning a change strategy

What was the leadership philosophy used, and the values placed
on people?

How would you describe the change: a planned evolution; a
short-term adaptation; a radical revolution?

What influencing strategy was used? Who and what were the
key levers for change?

What effort went into building a shared vision, ownership and
commitment?

Was change top-down, middle-out, or bottom-up?

How clear and measurable were the success criteria?

Overcoming resistance to change

What level of anticipation was there about potential issues with
regard to people's attitudes, climate and culture?

Were people positioned as potential blockers or enablers of change? What effort was made in capturing their hearts and minds?
How were blocks overcome?
What level of innovation emerges?

Positioning the role of HR

What role did HR take – the policy and support provider; the change facilitator; the change influencer; or change partner?
What factors most influenced the choice of HR's role?
What credibility challenges did HR have to overcome?

Resolving the personal dilemmas of the change influencer

What were the concerns uppermost in the change influencer's mind?
How did they resolve them?
What doubts and fears were evident?
How were they resolved?
How did they choose their own influencing style and approach?
   What constraints and boundaries did they put on themselves?
   How did they set about building a partnership in change with the line?
How would you describe the style chosen: the change visionary; facilitator; or influencer? What change leadership skills did you see them exhibiting?

Many of these questions would be highly pertinent to your planning and influencing of your company's change strategy. As a change leader and influencer you will need to develop your own check-list of thoughts.

The cases presented are from TSB, Reckitt & Colman; UK Paper; Smurfit Composites; Allied–Distillers; the Quicks Group;

Do-It-All; Courage Breweries and Grattans. A wide spectrum of businesses, spanning the banking, pharmaceutical, paper and packaging, wines and spirits, motor retailing, DIY, brewing and home shopping sectors. Company sizes range from 200 to 90,000 people. A rich menu is presented which will allow you to benchmark yourself and your company against the challenges faced.

The case providers did not sit down and write a comprehensive case history; as busy managers, that is not how they see or plan change. The structures given to the case-studies are ours, and were determined by interviewing the HR managers and directors involved. Their feedback was that they enjoyed and themselves learnt from both our interviews and the eventual construct of the cases presented. We wonder whether in the organisation of the future more time will be spent on building up a change leadership track record through continuous learning.

In presenting the cases, we have sought to emphasise different change leadership issues. In Chapter 11 we seek to illustrate how HR has sought to position itself as a strategic partner with the business, using the material from TSB and Reckitt & Colman. In Chapter 12 we present the cases in the form of an interview, and so aim to emphasise the change influencer's thinking processes. Here we use the UK Paper and Smurfit Composite cases. In Chapter 13 we present a whole array of short case-studies which illustrate a portfolio of change initiatives that HR can take. Here we use the Allied–Distillers, Quicks Group, Do-It-All, Courage Breweries and Grattans cases.

As researchers and learners ourselves, we are sure that you will find the cases to be insightful, especially if you think about the process of change leadership and influencing as distinct from the detailed background content.

11

HR as a Strategic Partner

Within this chapter we present two case-studies from TSB and Reckitt & Colman which demonstrate, in very practical terms, how the HR teams have been able to move their roles away from the traditional HR services position to that of strategic partners with the business. Examples which demonstrate the change leadership and influencing approach are used. The two cases differ in business focus: in TSB the emphasis is on competitive advantage through valuing people in a banking sector which is still in the throes of major rationalisation; whereas in Reckitt & Colman the emphasis is on building an HR strategy to support worldwide business growth ambitions.

Case-study: Reckitt & Colman Products Worldwide Pharmaceuticals

Formulating an HR strategy to support worldwide growth ambitions

Reckitt & Colman is a £2,000m business operating on a worldwide basis, being particularly strong in the UK, USA, South Africa, France and Australia, and employing some 20,000 people. Its core businesses are in household products – with key brands including Harpic, Airwick, Haze and Windolene; and OTC Pharmaceutical Products – with key brands of Dettol, Gaviscan, Lemsip and Fybogel. In 1995 a major group-wide review of overall strategy and performance was undertaken. A key outcome was to focus on the worldwide growth of the pharmaceutical business.

This case-study focuses on the impact of the worldwide pharmaceutical ambitions on the traditional UK core strength of the business. It is presented from the perspective of Trevor

Clark, the UK HR Manager who was a member of the UK lead team striving to shape the UK role and strategy within the emerging worldwide business. It is a story which vividly demonstrates the positioning of the HR role as a strategic partner within the business, a substantial shift away from the traditional HR role. Trevor Clark was determined to ensure that HR had an influential role in addressing the major changes required. The shifts he envisaged are set out in Figure 9.

The concept of 'People really making the difference' was the fundamental building block against which an overall group-wide business transformation and culture change strategy had been launched. Trevor's intent was to use this as a lever for enabling the UK team to consider the fit between business and HR strategy.

The overall business context

To understand the change leadership agenda that the pharmaceutical business faced, it is important to put this against the backcloth of the Reckitt & Colman group transformation strat-

Figure 9

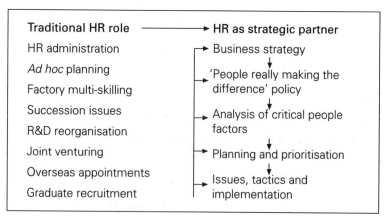

egy and the implications for the HR strategy for the pharmaceutical business.

Within the strategic review process a key insight emerging was of the need to develop a new mind-set and culture. This required a coherent statement of the group-wide mission and values – a value statement which emphasised that people together would 'really make the difference' to both the business transformations required and also to the future performance of the worldwide business.

In our terms of change leadership, this commitment to people by the top 50 directors and senior managers was a fundamental and public building-block. The business transformation envisaged required a major shift from running the business regionally towards co-ordinating the future strategy and direction for the business against identified global brands. The transformation agenda is shown in Figure 10.

Figure 10

The transformation agenda

> - Think globally and not locally.
> - Work through global teams and transfer expertise to better serve our consumers and customers.
> - Organise ourselves to think and work globally.
> - Seek product and innovation excellence.
> - Manage our business processes to serve our customers and consumers.
> - Staff the business with experts in chosen fields.

Within this plan a key challenge was thrown down to the top 50 to reconsider and develop their own leadership skills.

The prime focus was around the rationalisation of the worldwide household business to achieve global leadership. Many of the regional companies had been in both household and pharmaceuticals. The challenge to the newly created worldwide pharmaceuticals team was to create a distinctive and separate strategic focus.

The challenge to the worldwide pharmaceutical business

Pharmaceuticals had always been a different animal, with its long-term focus on R&D, new product development (NPD) and therapeutic illness trends, as distinct from the household business which needed to respond more quickly to competitive trends and consumer needs. Across pharmaceuticals much work had already been done to establish a distinctive corporate identity and culture. The announcement of the creation of a global pharmaceutical business formalised the planning and thinking that was already under way.

From the perspective of the UK team, the global ambition was a two-edged sword. On the one hand, the visible commitment to the pharmaceutical business's global potential was a measure of the success earned through the endeavours of the UK business. Yet this would require an aggressive build-up of the business in emerging 'tiger' economies of east and south Asia and Latin America. For the UK, they were now being made to see their role as part of a network of businesses as distinct from their traditional position as a prime business unit. Many concerns were beginning to emerge about the loss of UK power, influence and even future investment.

Trevor diagnosed that there were many people-issues needing to be addressed, not at a tactical but at a strategic level. His view was that reassurance wasn't needed, but clear strategic direction and clarity of intent. In this way, people could see how they were to fit into the grand scheme, especially around their own career prospects and future. He sought and won the agreement of his UK lead team colleagues that this was the right way forward. Trevor, with our help, decided to put together an overall HR strategy linked to the business strategy which addressed all of the key people-implications.

The UK organisation was faced with a number of major dilemmas, not only being the key profit generator but also the centre of brand and marketing know-how. To become a partner within a network of global businesses would require a major

Figure 11
UK NBU HR strategy

A BUSINESS ORGANISATION IN TRANSITION	
Away from ⟶ Towards	
• UK as self-standing business	• UK as a member of a WW pharmaceutical NBU network
• Focus on UK strategy	• Focus on WW category/regional strategy
• Control over UK manufacturing	• European lead manufacturing centres
• Dedicated R&D and NPD resources	• WW R&D resource delivering a WW NPD portfolio
• Country management accountability for pharmaceuticals and household	• WW pharmaceutical management structure
• Functional roles and responsibilities	• Multi-roles Category/function/region
• UK category management	• WW global category management
• UK profit generation	• Funding regional growth strategy
Independence ⟶ Strategic partnerships	

WW = Worldwide; NBUs = National Business Units

transition in UK thinking. The scale of the transitions faced is illustrated in Figure 11.

The development of the concept of a business in transition was a key insight, developed by Trevor and ourselves, which

Figure 12

Organic growth	New market development
• UK business plans *plus* • Category knowledge and professional network selling into NBU (WW)	• New channels and professional networks *plus* • International marketing know-how
New product development	Step out
• UK NPD needs in developed market *plus* • NPD applications into NBU (WW) and regional markets	• Licensing (UK) • Strategic alliances • UK synergies *plus* • European synergies • Licensing (WW)

allowed the UK lead team to view the future constructively, as distinct from being concerned about loss of power and influence; in particular, the idea of building a network of 'strategic partnerships' on a global basis. To ensure that the business fit for the HR strategy was evident, this was presented around the four-box business-planning matrix. (See Figure 12.)

From this strategic framework we took this thinking forward to address all of the potential people implications, resulting in a 'making the difference' (MTD) strategy.

An MTD HR strategy

Key Strategic Elements:

- Worldwide/UK business integration
- UK strategic focus
- resource planning
- MTD competency development
- career planning
- organisation culture
- motivation, reward and retention
- performance and productivity

- attracting, recruiting, promoting MTD talent
- change leadership.

This was presented to the UK lead team and the worldwide pharmaceutical marketing director. The response was very positive, with Trevor's colleagues being very surprised that HR had developed a strategic focus; a significant change from HR's historical image and reputation.

However, the news was not all good, as Trevor's plan had been to ask for priorities under all of the HR policy area headings for the next two or three years. This question unearthed the real issues that the team was worried about:

- the UK role within the emerging worldwide business structure
- their influence, authority and impact on future planning and policy making
- their freedoms to develop a UK strategy in what had been a hands-on, short-term culture.

A subteam of the lead team was created to address these issues and the implications for HR strategy. This involved Trevor, ourselves, Justin Lord, the European marketing director, and Stafford Dow, the UK sales director. It was a case of 'back to the drawing board', with the initial grand design rightly put on hold. This involvement of the line in partnership with HR was central to the next step, a business challenge to HR wisdom. The concept of HR strategy confused them and didn't seem to fit with their operational focus, especially at the time of year when budgets were being considered with the pressure on for delivery next year. A key breakthrough here was the linking of the strategic business agenda (see Figure 13) with a statement of the HR requirements to deliver competitive advantage:

> *The business need*: strategies for competitive advantage
>
> *HR strategic response*: Developing people who have the competencies in leading, managing and delivering to make the difference to the business agenda.

Figure 13 *Strategic business agenda*

Organic growth	New market development
• costs/margins • brands • channel strategy • professional networks	• new channel development • professional recommender networks
New product development	Step out
• programme focus • innovation • delivery	• joint ventures • contracting out • licensing in/out

and then matching these with competencies required in each of the business planning sectors (see Figure 14).

Our proposition was that different planning sectors required a different business focus, leadership style and distinctive competencies.

Figure 14 *Strategies for competitive advantage*

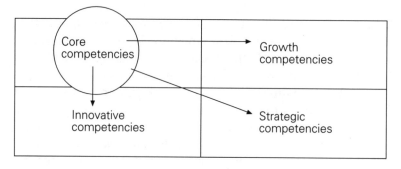

Organic growth (for example)

Business Focus: optimising performance
                   market share
                   costs and margins.
Leadership: clear goals and priorities
                   well-defined policies and procedures
                   devolved authorities

Competencies: in-depth brand, market, consumer and
                        competitive knowledge
                     squeezing performance out of tight
                        control and detail-mindedness.

New product development (NPD)

Business Focus: strategic NPD pipeline
                     integrating brand strategies,
                        technological strengths and
                        therapeutic trends.
Leadership: strategic focus and partnerships between
                        R&D and marketing.
Competencies: trend analysis
                     identifying unmet needs
                     strategic focus
                     innovation.

This framework enabled the business managers to recognise
that if the business was to grow rapidly from its current base
then, in HR planning terms, people with distinctive competencies would be needed who could 'make the difference' in each of
the planning sectors. This approach required an HR strategy
concerned with 'competitive competency development', 'future
resource allocation', 'leadership style and culture', and 'introducing a new value and reward set which motivated and recognised people for different strengths and contributions'. All of
which further reinforced the need for a strategic focus, a higher
level of management team time to address the people issues, and
the need for strategic, as distinct from operational, leadership.

These insights are now being integrated into the strategic
planning and resource allocation round. The debate has now
shifted from HR strategy to one of UK business strategy which
drives the need for an HR strategy to deliver competitive
advantage.

Lessons on change leadership

From Trevor's standpoint, the key lessons emerging are:

- the need for a strategic HR focus. Traditionally HR would have addressed the specific issues and not taken a strategic overview. This initiative raised the overall business need for clarity on strategy.
- the importance of HR acting as a strategic partner. Trevor's position on the UK lead team allowed him to demonstrate his business and commercial acumen, and from this base to help the team to address the people issues.
- that business strategy should lead the HR strategy. The HR strategy initiative forced the need for a coherent UK business strategy. From this, the notion of business growth and competitive advantage through people became the shared HR and business agenda.
- the need for joint line/HR shaping of strategy. The involvement of the line, with their business agenda and personal leadership approaches, highlighted the conceptual gaps which can occur between well-meaning HR people and the line.
- the need for an evolutionary, as distinct from radical, approach. A step-by-step building of HR strategy, against perceived and felt needs, proved to be much more successful than laying out a grand design. For HR to shift from a service role to a strategic role is an efficient challenge in itself for the line; the realisation was that they had never had the chance to think HR strategy before, and that a major educational input was required.

Against our model of change leadership

The change visionary competencies

The recognition that the UK business was a business in transition was a central part of the initial diagnosis, especially when this was set against the issues of global ambitions and organisation.

— the scanning and interrogating competencies.

The initiative to shape an HR strategy and then to link it with business strategy was fundamental.

— the shaping competencies.

The change influencing competencies

The diagnosis of the issues to be faced in people terms raised the agenda from an operational to a strategic level.

— the standing-apart competencies.

These insights succeeded in demonstrating the HR competencies and also broadened the thinking processes. The credibility earned was a key to committing high-level management time to the HR strategic considerations.

— the organisation-influencing competencies.

The change facilitation competencies

The initial intent was to take the steam out of fears about the loss of UK power and influence and replace those by the concept of strategic, influential partners. This valuing of people's expertise and knowledge to influence thinking was a key to the constructive response.

— the empathising competencies.

Credit is due to Trevor Clark for his insights and determination that HR should be a credible strategic partner. Also to Justin Lord and Stafford Dow, who brought us back to earth and ensured that business and HR strategy were properly linked.

Case-study: TSB Group plc

Delivering competitive advantage and sustaining customer loyalty through valuing people to 'make the difference'

TSB, like all of the major banks, has gone through a substantial period of organisational restructuring and business process re-engineering, a high level of investment in technology, a differentiation between the front office as a customer service centre and the back office as a regionalised administration centre, plus a substantial degree of downsizing. All of this has been aimed at creating improved customer service and competitive income/cost ratios compared with the other major high street banks. This restructuring process had been substantially achieved by the end of 1995. The price paid was in employee motivation, morale and, inevitably, loyalty.

For TSB the important challenge was to rebuild employee loyalty and hence ensure customer loyalty, and beyond that to strive for enhanced competitive advantage through people, in terms of the search for continuous improvement in service, responsiveness to market change, and innovation in products and services.

This case-study represents the work done in 1995 by Peter Hessey, director of HR strategy, and his team. The foundations laid will inevitably have a substantial impact on the successful integration of Lloyds TSB, a major merger which was announced in 1995.

The battle for customer loyalty

In banking, customer loyalty and retention are key factors, especially in a business environment under threat from building societies and insurance companies. The battle for customers in a converging bank-insurance sector required clear plans to secure the existing customer base, to deliver outstanding customer service via technology, and then to grow via innovative product service development.

The trigger for this strategic stocktaking on customer loyalty was a series of executive management team discussions around the impact of employee loyalty on the 'service–profit chain'. An early reference in laying down this challenge was the work done by James L Heskett, *et al,* in the *Harvard Business Review,* March 1996, 'Putting the Service–Profit Chain to Work'. Their research had identified a number of powerful tenets around 'customer loyalty':

Customer and employee loyalty

- Customer loyalty drives profitability and growth.
- Customer satisfaction drives customer loyalty.
- Value drives customer satisfaction.
- Employee productivity drives value.
- Employee loyalty drives productivity.
- Employee satisfaction drives loyalty.
- Internal quality drives employee satisfaction.
- Leadership shapes a quality service culture and inspires employees.

This challenge was thrown down to the HR team and picked up by Peter Hessey in his HR strategy role. In straightforward terms, the questions asked were:

- Where are we now?
- Where do we need to be to sustain competitive advantage?
- Where do we fall short?
- What changes are needed?

Over and above this, the top team in TSB, the group executive committee (GEC), had set TSB on a course to achieve the mission:

> To become the leading UK financial retailer through under-standing and meeting our customer needs by being more professional and innovative than our competitors.

The achievement of this mission was to be against the set of corporate values illustrated in Figure 15.

Figure 15
TSB values

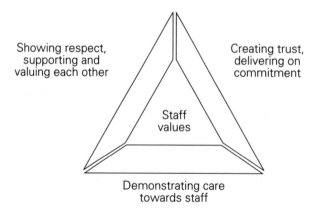

Building top management commitment

Peter Hessey, in discussion with his HR colleagues across the group, recognised that the shifts required a major culture change programme. This was further reinforced by the 1993 staff attitude survey. TSB carries out such surveys annually, which highlight 'low motivation and morale'.

The gap between the intention (see Figure 16) and the reality was self-evident when the results of the survey were made

Figure 16
The HR intention

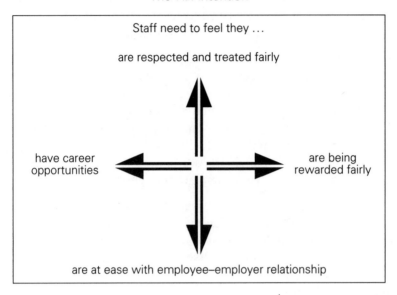

Staff need to feel they ...

are respected and treated fairly

have career opportunities

are being rewarded fairly

are at ease with employee–employer relationship

public. They reflected the impact of the scale of change on staff. Major challenges emerging in building a highly motivated workforce are shown in Figure 17.

Figure 17
Staff attitude survey – Sept–Oct 1993

Motivational challenges

- Future involvement with TSB
- Concern with job security
- Value placed on staff
- Future career prospects
- Openness on future business direction
- Greater understanding of decisions

A major presentation was made initially to the GEC and then to the top 50 managers across the group. The key message given by Peter was that if TSB wished to secure competitive advantage through people then TSB would need to embark on:

- a major culture change programme:
  - to rebuild employee motivation and confidence
  - to build commitment to and understanding of the practical realities of the TSB mission and values in action.
- a root and branch review of the TSB HR policy framework:
  - to ensure the policies facilitated the transformation in performance, behaviour, attitudes and competencies to deliver competitive advantage through people.

The top 50 planning conference was a crucial event, in that their support as the key leaders of the business was essential to lead the envisaged transformation process. The proposed HR strategy's objectives were endorsed by the conference.

HR resources strategy

Philosophy
The human resource function seeks to create an environment in which employees are able to maximise their contribution to the business objectives of quality, productivity, profitability and superior customer service.
    At the same time as contributing significantly to the business goals and objectives the function will ensure that all employees are treated with respect, dignity and fairness as they seek to meet their own individual aspirations.

HR strategic objectives

- to develop a strong organisation in which the people are capable of meeting the performance requirements of the business
- to continually upgrade the quality of managerial human resources in order to achieve a significant competitive advantage in the marketplace

- through dedication to excellence continually improve the quality and efficiency of non-management human resources in a changing and high technology environment in order to achieve customer service pre-eminence
- to develop a high level of staff morale and motivation and a positive employer-employee relationship which is based upon mutual respect and trust such that TSB is seen by all its staff as a 'preferred employer'.

The whole exercise was to be carried out under the banner of 'making the difference through people'.

Developing a strategy for competitive advantage through people

HR policy review

The plan was to carry out a root and branch review of all HR policy. A project management structure was established, involving the line and HR, with six major project steering groups. These were supported by a subteam structure working on specific aspects of the policy review, including benchmarking of best practice, desk research, discussions with leading academics and professional advisers. Some 18 teams were set up, all co-ordinated through a project management structure led by Peter. The policy review areas and key issues were:

- Motivation – managing business and culture change; instituting the stated values in action
- Resource planning – planning for the future and monitoring the development of the existing resource base
- Recruitment and selection – equipping the business with the people it needs, both now and into the future
- Succession planning – equipping our people to do their current and future jobs

- Reward and recognition – rewarding and recognising people for their contribution to both performance and the TSB values
- Retention – ensuring the retention of people we want by building and reinforcing the relationship with key people.

This review was to take some four to six months. Peter Hessey's role was to ensure that the interdependencies between the policy reviews were considered and that the whole package was in line with the overall business and HR mission. No mean task in an HR and line community which had very traditional views about the HR impact. Much challenge, education and lobbying was required to maintain the focus and momentum.

Culture change

We recognised together, early in our considerations, that major culture change would not result from changing HR policies alone. Somehow we had to find a framework which integrated all of the initiatives required. Key factors here were that:

- the mission and values exercise would need to be positioned as the strategic business focus around which the theme of 'making the difference through people' would be developed
- TSB had been through a major business process re-engineering exercise which had reorientated the organisation towards the key organisational processes. Some further restructuring was still envisaged around the impact of technology
- leadership behaviour and attitudes would be central and their willingness to challenge their behaviour and impact would be essential
- value statements always ran the risk of motherhood and clear workable processes would be needed to address 'values in action'.

From these considerations an integrative framework was developed which became the basis for planning the culture change strategy and also eventually for launching the culture change programme (see the figure in the Appendix, p. 208).

Values in action

The 'values in action' exercise was to be positioned as a team review process which would be cascaded into the organisation. With the support of the top 50 managers, the intent was that they should demonstrate a willingness to challenge their own team behaviour and performance and thus act as role models. The cascading of the reviews would mean that down each functional or business line a diagnosis of the needs for change would be made, coupled with a programme for improvement at the relevant organisational level.

Workbooks embracing all of TSB values were developed for these team reviews; elements of these workbooks are illustrated in Figure 18.

Leadership commitment to change

This comprehensive culture change package was presented to the top team in September 1995, after a process of discussion and planning with Peter Ellwood, the group chief executive, whose leadership and visible commitment were paramount. The strategy was endorsed; a key debate centred around which business should be included, and the policy agreed was for all TSB branded companies.

The next stage was to be another top 50 conference in October 1995. This was overtaken by the public announcement of the plan to merge Lloyds and TSB, which eventually happened in January 1996. For the HR team involved, this was a setback; however, the current wisdom is that many of the ideas developed will be highly relevant to the successful integration of Lloyds–TSB, which further accelerated the mission of becoming the leading financial services retailer.

Figure 18 *TSB 'values in practice'*

Value	Leadership practice	Actions	Results
1. *Being customer-focused*	1.1 Identify and continuously implement improved ways to anticipate, serve and satisfy internal and external customer needs	• With team determine internal and external customers • Develop processes to better understand and anticipate customer needs • Encourage 'service orientation' in team • Diagnose factors inhibiting good customer performance and plan improvements • Recognise and reward service improvements • Set service targets and standards	• Positive feedback from customers • Increased customer contact • Relationships will change to 'a partnership with customers' • Customers will play a more proactive role in determining service required • Service standards will improve
4. *'Being efficient'*	4.1 Stress the importance of developing and implementing more effective and efficient ways to improve procedures, products and services through a quality orientation	• Emphasise need to question and challenge procedures and systems • Assign task teams to seek performance improvements • Reward and recognise 'improvement achievements' • Constantly ask 'Can we do it better?' • Diagnose blocks to performance improvement, use task teams to overcome blocks • Establish clear performance and quality standards	• Decisions will be made on the basis of sound research and data • Old ways will be challenged • Bureaucracy will diminish • More regular and pertinent questions will be asked • Efficiency and effectiveness will have improved

Lessons on change leadership

From Peter Hessey's viewpoint, the key lessons were:

- the importance of the focus on competitive advantage through people. The insights on the correlation between customer loyalty, business performance and employee morale and motivation at the outset of the programme were fundamental.
- the need to drive the programme against a clear business strategy. The business rationale and objectives had to be the targets for culture change, especially in a performance-focused culture.
- the amount of time and resources required to put together a major review. TSB had developed a project management strength in terms of facing change. The HR reviews built on this.
- the effort required in communication and consultation for change to succeed in a large complex organisation. Commitment to change and understanding was required across the whole group. The initial planning phase would have been followed by a major change leadership education programme.
- the credibility building required for HR to establish itself as a strategic partner. The extensive planning work, the initial diagnosis, the 'making the difference through people' strategy, the business case for change, all served to earn credits and enhance HR's reputation. This exercise raised substantially the profile and standing of HR.

Against our model of change leadership

The change visionary competencies

The whole exercise was positioned around the need for a clear HR philosophy and strategy, culture change and the benefits to be accrued through people in terms of competitive advantage.

– the shaping competencies.

The linking of culture change strategy to envision of the business operations into the year 2000 and beyond took account of the marketplace trends, changing working practices, new concepts of organisation required, changing career expectations and employee psychological contracts.

– the scanning and interrogating competencies.

The change influencer competencies

The use of the employee survey data to hold the mirror up to management on the quality of employee loyalty and the impact on customer loyalty was a major challenge and an inescapable truth.

– the standing back and challenging competencies.

The extensive project group structure, the top team strategy review meetings, and the top 50 conferences were all an essential part of building a commitment to change. This was coupled with extensive one-to-one discussions with the TSB top team on their vision for the future.

– the organisation-influencing competencies.

The change facilitation competencies

The planning conferences highlighted the need for a clear and measurable business rationale within the overall strategy. This added to the initial HR focus.

– the open-minded competencies.

The line/HR project groups generated many ideas on the changes needed to deliver a TSB competitive advantage.

– the innovation competencies.

Our thanks are due to John Penny, the group HR director, for his business pragmatism and sense of reality which he brought to the plans to influence senior line management thinking and his initiative in creating a director of HR strategy role; and to Peter Hessey for allowing us to participate in the project and his willingness to share his thinking and insights in what was an extensive planning exercise for a major culture change programme. We see this case as an invaluable benchmark for other companies in the financial services sector who are still in the throes of continuous change and restructuring.

12

♟ Understanding the Dilemmas of HR as a Change Influencer

In our next case-studies, with UK Paper and Smurfit Composites, we have adapted an interview style of presentation. In doing this we have sought to search for a deeper understanding of the personal questions and dilemmas that the change influencer faces. For you, the responses given may well reflect the questions that go through your mind. If not, they will certainly add to your own planning of your change initiatives.

Case-study: UK Paper Limited

Introducing world-leading working practices on a 'brownfield' site

UK Paper is a leading manufacturer of wood-free fine papers. They were acquired in 1990 by Fletcher Challenge, a New Zealand-based conglomerate with a worldwide turnover of $4.4 billion. Their aim was to establish a market position in Europe. They were determined to introduce world-class working practices into a traditional industry.

Their target was the new recycled fibre plant, an investment of £43m, which was also in line with their environment protection policy in the recycling of office waste paper. This case-study covers the pioneering work undertaken by the newly appointed management team headed by Dave Haver, the general manager, and involving as change architects Peter Christmas, the operations manager, and Deborah Burt, the HR development manager.

The fascinating story told by Deborah Burt represents a thoroughly planned and fundamental approach to the introduction of new world-class working practices on a 'brownfield' site. This is case-study which vividly emphasises the real and substantial investment required to break out of traditional habits and thinking and to lay the foundations for a totally new style of operation, based on multi-skilled, self-managed teams.

The 'brownfield' opportunity

UK Paper was determined that the recycled pulp plant with the fine quality papers emerging represented a significant commercial opportunity. The view was that in strategic marketing terms a high performance, state-of-the-art plant would deliver cost advantages at the outset. A turnkey project was going to cost £40M; their only proviso was that the investment in state-of-the-art technology required the best operational and working practices.

The new management team was appointed to plan the start-up of this new plant. They were given a tight timetable of two years to research, benchmark, plan, recruit and train the total plant operations team and start up the operations. They were given the freedom to recruit a team of their own choice as distinct from having to fit in existing UK Paper employees.

They set about researching and benchmarking against the best practice plants across the Fletcher Challenges group. From this they recognised that it would be essential to match the state-of-the-art technology with a new philosophy of HR operating principles. Deborah Burt, who had initially been trained in New Zealand and Australia, was given the task of defining these principles. Her previous experience emphasised the importance of a clear vision and values statement. She visited other group plants and also other world-class manufacturing operations. From this research the following principles were defined and agreed.

To meet our members' needs:

- we will create a sense of belonging in an environment of mutual trust, respect and dignity
- we believe that all people want to be involved in decisions that affect them, care about their jobs, take pride in themselves and their contributions and want to share in the success of their efforts
- we will develop the tools, training and education for each member, recognising individual skills and knowledge
- we believe that creative, motivated and responsible team members who understand that change is critical to success are UK Paper's most important asset.

These principles were fundamental to the intention to establish a culture which valued people, continuous personal learning, teamworking, openness and involvement, and continuous change and improvement. These principles were used in the design of an innovative team-based management structure.

Building a vision of the new organisation

In our discussion with Deborah Burt we posed the following change leadership questions.

How did the management team set about defining such a novel style of operation?

They initially had to look at the technical viability of substituting recycled fibre for virgin wood fibres, because as a plant it was to be the first of its kind in the world. They set out to benchmark best operating practices by visiting mills in the USA, Canada and all over Europe. They concluded that they wished to introduce a team style of operation, which was the only steer they gave me.

How did you set about defining this team concept?

My initial diagnosis was that in the existing Sittingbourne mills they operated very hierarchically, with a large number of management levels, including shift supervisors and operators who did just one task, with little communication. It was a very traditional industry. We realised early on the scale of change we faced.

I spent two months doing benchmark research. I spoke to companies in the States and New Zealand and to external consultants. I sought out articles on teamworking, and explored what best practice companies were doing. From all of this I painted a picture of the operating principles and practices needed.

How did you set about influencing the management team's thinking?

Initially, when I came across an exciting new idea which I believed would work for us I raised it. We spent a lot of time bouncing off ideas together. Examples were circles on organisation charts; the concepts of multi-skilling; job rotation; continuous training support. They saw me as a dog with a bone. They could see more barriers than I did in a traditional environment.

I had a wide scope. They were building trust in me; they saw me as responsible for the people dimension of the plan. They focused on the technical and commercial aspects, while I addressed people and culture.

The outcome of this process of research and benchmarking, idea sharing and testing is illustrated in Table 1 which highlights the scale of change from historical, conventional practice.

The next challenge was to set about recruiting for the new organisation. The intention was to start with a new workforce and build the operational practices together. A 'greenfield' approach to a 'brownfield' site.

Table 1 *The scale of change from conventional practice*

Organisation job skills		Management information (IT)	
From	*To*	*From*	*To*
• Single accountability • Supervisor does work schedules • Layers • Functional specialisation • Many individual pay grades	• Team accountability • Supervisor as coach • Flat structure • Multi-skilled • Behavioural competence > technical	• Mainly financial • Operational by special study • IT specialists • Manual records • Non-integrated • My data is better	• Operational open to all • Wide IT literacy open access • Data management • Plant-wide • Groupwide

Management systems		Culture	
From	*To*	*From*	*To*
• Act on financials • Low frequency of reporting • Data held by functional groups • Not process • Top-down appraisal	• Act on customer • Daily, available to all • Whole process • Continuous improvement • 360° appraisal • Team rewards	• Not invented here • Hierarchical/directive • Functional walls • Information is power • Status symbols	• Action learning • Low blame • Empowered • Exhaustive consultation • All issues dealt with • High challenge/high support

Building the new organisation

How did you set about building the new organisation?

In terms of our recruitment process we decided to use assessment centres. We defined the technical skills and competency profiles required for the team roles. Over 1,500 people applied, including some 35 from the existing operations. For the internal candidates, we invited them over to explain what we were about and then interviewed them all. We ended up taking eight of them into a new organisation of 40 people.

At our assessment centres we did psychometric and ability testing, and team exercises to observe their team skills. We had three days of assessment centres for 75, out of which we chose 30. We wanted to recruit a pool of people for the operators and team co-ordinator jobs. We planned to delay the appointment of team co-ordinators until after the training programme. The intention was that for every successful candidate, personal feedback should be given to them on their skills profile. The feedback from the candidates was that everyone felt that it was both a novel and fair system.

The framework of competencies and skills required is illustrated in Table 2. The breadth of the qualities sought was essential in building a world-class operation. It is interesting to note the emphasis given to the balance of skills across technical and personal skills.

Induction training

How did you set about introducing this pool of people to what was a very innovative concept?

We had to take these people's backgrounds, their personal luggage and experience, to challenge and educate them against what we wanted to achieve. We set up HR training, to create a culture and environment. We wanted to equip them with skills like

Table 2 *Key competencies for technical operating staff*

Key technical skills	
• Engineering aptitude	an aptitude for engineering and science-based disciplines
• Diagnostic/problem-solving	an ability to understand industrial equipment, diagnose problems and find solutions
• Numerical aptitude	level of numeracy sufficient to handle routine statistics, quality control and administrative procedures.
Key personal skills	
• Team orientation	a good team member, willing to make a contribution to the success of the team without being overdependent on a team environment
• Self-management	has sufficient confidence and maturity to work by him/herself when necessary
• Flexibility	willingness to accept and adopt new ideas and work practices without being dogmatic
• Leadership potential	commands respect and is listened to by others. Has the ability to achieve results through the efforts of others.
Other skills or abilities	
• Driving	a key element of the job for many of the operators will be the ability to drive heavy vehicles, particularly fork-lift trucks
• Chemistry and electronics	knowledge of both subjects would be a significant advantage
• Physical fitness	must be able-bodied without any limitations. Good depth perception necessary for operating fork lift trucks in limited space.

problem-solving, leadership and teamworking as well as getting to know each other. We also wanted them to explore their own profiles, their strengths and weaknesses, their own comfort zones and personal ambitions. We really wanted to challenge them as a group.

How did they respond to all of this, in what for many would be seen as a radically different approach?

At the start they were very passive. We had spent two years planning, so I suppose we were selling the benefits. They were sceptical at first; it was very unnerving and quite exposing.

How did you deal with that?

We kept a close eye on the situation, and dealt with issues as they arose. We recognised that we had to go through the pain of 'unlearning'. We wanted to let them learn for themselves and be educated.

Was this not a process of imposition?

Yes, it was. But we wanted people who wished to learn and develop; if not, our team concept wouldn't succeed. We decided to start with a technical skills development programme for each individual, eg in electrical, instrumental, hydraulics, safety and computing. We put them into three groups for skills training. Those who were in the trade, those new to the industry, and finally the graduate group who had the theory but no practical experience. Each person's skills development was regularly reviewed. They were to have some six months of training.

This is an exceptional investment: who funded it?

In terms of our start-up plan, we had agreed with the parent company a training budget of around £150,000.

Defining the new operations

After the training, what was the next phase of organisation building?

We set up a series of mixed teams to address how the plant would operate in practice. We had teams on shift patterns, operating manuals, clothing, safety, communication and other aspects of the new operations. They had to go out and benchmark, come up with ideas and own them. They sent out questionnaires to local and best-practice companies. Their task was to come up with proposals in which they believed.

What was the role of the management team throughout all of this?

The management team saw itself as a support team. What actually mattered was what the total team of 35 people wanted to do in terms of running the plant. The management was a guiding force which ensured that the people could do their jobs to the best of their ability. The teams came up with proposals which initially went for the cheap options, because of past experience. We pushed them towards coming up with the best solution for our problems, and the best business decisions. We were determined that world-class operations would emerge from the commitment of the operating teams.

How innovative were they?

They developed their own electronic newsletter, called *Pulp Fiction*. They came up with a shift pattern for our continuous operations which matched their needs where they worked only one weekend in five. Interestingly, now that the system is running, they are beginning to complain. We turned it back on them and said it's your shift pattern: if want to change it, review it with your colleagues.

Selecting the team co-ordinators

All of these 'virtual' teams had a key part to play in the building of the new team culture and practices. The next challenge was to create the formal team structures and appoint the team co-ordinators.

How did you select the co-ordinators?

We initially sat down as a management team to make the decisions but quickly decided to put the ball in their court. We gave them some guidelines: the team leaders were to be co-ordinators of people, processes, resources and information. They were not to be directive but facilitative. The teams were to be the sources of the skills needed. They decided that they wished to call the role 'team co-ordinator'. They voted for individuals. We were pleased that they came up with 'people people'. This was an important statement, as they were paid £4,000 more than the team members.

How did you feel about this?

We were very encouraged, because their choices matched the principles we were pursuing.

The role of the management team as change leaders

This case-study vividly demonstrates a real commitment to a devolved style of self-managed team operations. For the management team, brought up in traditional management methods, the whole process must have been very tough and demanding. A key question, inevitably, concerned their capacity to respond to these new challenges.

How did they cope with not being the traditional manager, making the decisions?

They went through the HR training with the pool of operators. They wanted to demonstrate that things were going to be different. They didn't wish to divorce themselves from the team process. As individuals, they acknowledged their own management style and baggage, they were conscious of the need not to display that. They strove to feed information down, give them ownership, and back off. This was difficult because they were aware of their tendencies to be directive and interfere.

We spend a lot of time reviewing our behaviour and challenging each other. They saw me as the challenging conscience of our HR principles and values.

We were determined that our actions and behaviours would match the stated intent. We reviewed the projects weekly. We reviewed people and how they were progressing against the strategy. We were reviewing, amending, building and improving all the time. We reiterated every two months our vision and the progress against the overall start-up timetable. We did this openly and publicly.

What encouraged you to believe that your strategy was on track?

A highlight in the building of the team identity and culture was a visit by everybody to our operations in Ravensburg in Germany. It was a benchmarking visit. Everybody said it was the best team-building event they had been on, radically different from their previous experience.

Also, we are now beginning to see the signs of being challenged by the rest of the overall team. The team co-ordinators represent the views of their teams; want to take ownership of the actions needed. If we interfere, they are beginning to challenge us back.

The whole process appears to be very thorough and apparently with no major hitches; was that really the case?

We have had a number of hitches. In the early days people could not believe in the level of investment in training. They assumed it would end. I had to say, 'if you want to develop, we have made a commitment and the funds will be there'. They found this truly hard to believe.

We currently have a major crisis. The plant is not working; we are late; the mills won't take our product; this is demotivating for us all. There is mistrust from our customers. The market is tough and so we cannot compromise on quality.

The problems are technical. The team was up and ready but everything is on hold. We are completely honest with them, we communicate regularly, seek ideas. The management team has had to insist that the focus should be on the longer term rather than teething problems. It is very difficult and a real test of our philosophy.

The role of HR

These developments illustrate the importance of planning and benchmarking. The 'brownfield' start-up illustrates the scale of the organisation-building and innovative culture development programme. It raises a number of fundamental insights about the role and influence of HR required.

How would you describe the role that HR has played?

From the outset my role has been to focus on the people processes. The managers saw their task as being concerned with the project's technical and commercial aspects. Once we had built mutual trust and understanding, they treated me as a partner in the process.

At the management team level, the 'behaviour checks' were seen as uncomfortable, but necessary. With the operator teams, my role has been to reinforce our vision and commitment to the HR principles; to challenge and confront the doubts raised; to act as the team's conscience; to be very visible and available throughout each stage of the process.

I spent time on the shop floor, talking to and listening to people. This has been commented on, with remarks like, 'in my old factory management would never have done that. This was very encouraging to us.'

Lessons on change leadership

What then are the lessons you draw about change leadership?

- The importance of planning up-front. To be clear in your mind what you want to achieve and to ensure the buy-in and support of senior management. This is essential.

- We underestimated the need for facilitators. For anyone going through a major change programme, the number and skills of the change facilitators are key.
- The importance of a contingency plan, especially if things do not go to plan. The extension and delay in the start-up has given us real problems.
- The value of benchmarking as a learning tool, the exposure and visioning is very important.
- I have learned a lot about myself, the need for patience, the art of influencing, to never assume – especially about people.
- The need to be realistic. If the aim is to be world-class, they need to investigate, have a clear strategy, review and continuously learn and adapt. There has to be a consciousness to achieving world-class status.

All of this demonstrates the thoroughness and clarity of values required in the change partner role.

Against our model of change leadership

The change visionary competencies

A central theme of the whole case has been the desire to research, benchmark and learn from others. This unending search to define and understand the concept of world-class is vivid.

> – *the scanning and interrogating competencies.*

The success of the organisation start-up was achieved by coherent planning with a shared vision on the HR principles to be followed. Living those principles in practice has been central to the 'behaviour challenge'.

> – *the visioning and shaping competencies.*

The change influencer competencies

HR played a fundamental role in building the new organisation, not only as champions of the vision but also in standing back, observing and challenging the drift from the intended principles in practice.

   – *the standing apart and challenging competencies.*

The building of the new organisation around the concept of interdependent teams required a clear focus on the whole being greater than the sum of the parts. Management has needed and wanted 'behaviour checks' to play their part. The teams have needed reassurance that the real commitment was there and not just words on paper. The role of HR as the 'organisation's conscience' has been crucial.

   – *the organisation-influencing competencies.*

The change facilitator competencies

The whole programme of training and investment in people has been substantial. The value placed on people and their potential to grow, take part and be innovative is very evident. The devolution of responsibility to build the operating practices is clear evidence of the trust placed in people.

   – *the openness to the views of others competencies.*

The pay-off from the start has been the ownership taken and the quality of the idea generation. This, coupled with holding people accountable for their own recommendations in practice, was key learning.

   – *the stimulation of innovation competencies.*

We wish to thank Dave Haver, the general manager and Peter Christmas, the operations manager at UK Paper for allowing us to learn from their experience. Our particular thanks go to Deborah Burt, on what was her first major change assignment, for her observations, openness, insights and passion about change leadership 'consciousness'. Her story is a model for others who wish to be change influencers based on the recognition of the need to learn and grow oneself.

Case-study: Smurfit Composites

Introducing culture change into a traditional manufacturing site in west Cumbria

This case-study is an illustration of the implications of the impact of a new owner, a world-class company with a clear set of corporate values and principles, on a traditional manufacturing outpost on the coast of west Cumbria. It describes the impact of a new owner's philosophy on the workforce, the management team and, more specifically, the HR function.

The story, as it unfolds, demonstrates the ripple effect of change and the dilemmas raised by applying a new philosophy to a traditional, hierarchical manufacturing site; it highlights the risks and benefits involved in pursuing a philosophy of greater openness and involvement on a site which, in terms of both business and manufacturing technology, was going through substantial change. A substantial change leadership challenge, where the greater automation and the upgrading of manufacturing technology will produce greater line efficiencies but will, at the same time, put at risk the traditional jobs, particularly in an environment where the new owner's philosophy has encouraged the workforce to take more responsibility for its own development and personal growth.

The factory, on the outskirts of Whitehaven in west Cumbria, was acquired by the Jefferson Smurfit Group. This Group is a world-leading packaging products business which operates over 350 plants in 14 countries worldwide. They convert paper and board produced at 15 mills into a whole variety of packaging products for the retail and manufacturing sectors across the world.

The programme of change is described from the perspective of Phylis McKain, the HR manager, who was given personal responsibility to drive through culture change on the back of an Investors in People programme. Her story is one of a corporate-wide initiative and directive, having the positive side effect of moving HR from the traditional personnel services role towards one of creating the potential to become a business partner. It demonstrates the need for a dogged and pragmatic approach to change, away from the sophisticated concepts of culture and corporate values towards dealing with the realities of breaking down old attitudes in a highly practical way, eg, in terms of educating people that training is not just about attending courses, but also to do with personal, on-the-job development.

The business need

The Jefferson Smurfit business philosophy is based on sub-stantial and successful growth over the last 60 years. The Jefferson Smurfit Group began as a small boxmaker in Ireland in 1934, was publicly quoted in 1964 and is now one of the major paper-based packaging companies in the world, which in the last seven years has resulted in some 20 acquisitions across Europe. The Group is now No. 1 in the world in container board, corrugated containers, paper reclamation and folding cartons, with total managed sales of £6,778m in Ireland and $10,155m in the US. Their business philosophy, 'the Smurfit way', is based around the concept of managing for continuous improvements (MFCI), and is stated:

> Our objective is to sell to our customers products that conform to their requirements, on time, at a competitive price. We do this by providing the encouragement and the means for continuous improvements in our processes, tech-nology, products and services. In this endeavour we are

committed to working with the highest standards of ethics
in a team-like manner, bringing credit to ourselves, our
shareholders and our community.

For the newly acquired Smurfit Composites factory in Cumbria,
a traditionally-run operation, the new owner with its success and
high ideals presented both a major challenge and opportunity.
Reflecting on the programme of change over last year Phylis
McKain, when asked, 'What really made the difference to your
change process?', replied by saying:

> They (Smurfit) are much more open, and encourage com-
> munication. You feel as if you are more involved. With our
> previous owners we were a little bleep in the corner of west
> Cumbria. Nobody was really interested in us. In the past, as
> long as money came in, that was fine, but they weren't
> really investing in us. Since Smurfit took over we feel
> much more involved, that we have a role to play and they
> are willing to talk to and listen to us.

These were the foundations on which change was to be built.

As the new owner, Smurfit initiated a number of key
actions:

- a review of the business plan
- an investment programme in the new technology, and the
  introduction of new working practices
- the introduction of the managing for continuous improvement
  programme (MFCI) – based on BS5750 accreditation, the
  introduction of an Investors in People scheme and an investment in national vocational qualification awards.

All of this was done in the middle of major recession in the UK,
with the commensurate pressure on UK sales and costs and the
need to shift the focus to export business.

Launching a culture change programme

Phylis was given the direct responsibility for the successful
introduction of the Investors in People and the NVQ schemes; it
was the first time she had ever tackled a project of that size.

What was going through your mind when you were given that task?

> I was terrified. The task was first put in the management team's hands and then just passed over to me. When I actually sat down to think it through, I thought: how on earth am I going to achieve all of this?

What terrified you?

> The sheer amount of work to be done and that I knew I had to change everybody's attitude. At that time on the shop floor nobody believed that anyone had invested in them or trained them.

How did you set about changing people's minds?

> Initially we used a Smurfit Group consultant on Investors in People. We did a case-study on what we were doing at that time and the changes needed to meet the criteria for the award. The outcome of this review was that we would have to introduce an appraisal scheme, induction training, a new training-needs analysis and a budget for training. We also needed to decide what was in line with our business plan.

What was the link between the business plan and training?

> It was all to do with BS5750 – a focus on quality and investment in people, who are our biggest asset. We had to do a lot of retraining because we were introducing new machinery and flexible working. We reached agreement with our unions that everybody would be trained and developed in all aspects of the shop floor work.

Was this a difficult discussion with the unions?

> No, they were receptive. They recognised that this was the way forward. We had a good relationship with the union representatives. We talked to them about everything, about taking people on and letting people go. Smurfit talked to the unions; they shared their plans and sought comment.

We consulted with them and expected them to co-operate, which they did.

Going back to the initial case-study, and all of the actions required for the award, what was the top management's reaction?

They recognised that their perception of good people-management in the past, when viewed against the criteria, was really 'lip service'.

How did they respond to this challenge?

We had to go for BS5750, for Investors in People, and the MFCI programme. It was a group policy to encourage participation in these projects.

How was this policy tuned to the needs of your factory?

That was my role. It involved all this change, as far as the workforce was concerned. I had to decide the way forward. We introduced voluntary NVQs on the shop floor. Encouragingly, some 26 people from the 80 on the shop floor were interested. We started at the machine process skills level. This year we went into business administration and information technology. We also did supervisory level III training.

What were you trying to achieve by the NVQ scheme? Were you trying to change the role of the first line management?

In the first place, we were trying to give them a better idea of the benefits of NVQs. My view was that they broadened people's outlooks. Topics like managing people, good relationships as well as getting a job done, eg, health and safety and its link to good housekeeping and how they are responsible for this. In essence, creating a new attitude of saying, 'it's not the boss's fault but my personal responsibility'.

To support this we also have training officers on the line, who are empowered to deal with all aspects of training, from induction to performance. They produce the training sheets. Managers will now go out and audit the needs on each other's lines. In the past, HR did all of this.

We also encourage people to decide for themselves, whether they are trained or not. They are made responsible for their own development and have to do their own training sheets.

Do you find that the same people are wanting more training?

Yes, I am afraid so. We have now had to put their training on hold until we sort out our future plans and structure of the company.

How has management responded to this ground swell of interest in personal development from the shop floor?

They have responded very well, supporting many of the training projects suggested by the shop floor. We tend to pilot simple things, eg, kinetic handling, to do with training people how to lift and carry things. We brought this in as part of the health and safety culture.

What other initiatives did you take, over and above the NVQ scheme?

We launched a series of communication meetings, where the management team would meet with about 16 to 20 of the workforce. We would speak about both good and bad news, what was happening in our company and in the total organisation. We raised topics like BS5750, Investors in People, training and development, health and safety; we encouraged questions and answers, which raised a lot of interest.

How successful was this?

Sadly, we realised that this was taking up too much production time: about six hours per month. We had to reduce the briefings to three times a year. To compensate for this we now do a monthly newsletter, with input from both management and shop floor.

We also ran MFCI workshops for small groups, where all their ideas were bandied about.

What were the exciting ideas raised?

People were happy to move about in jobs, very different from the historic view that 'this is my job and nobody else is going to do it'. They felt more recognised and so they responded. There were lots of practical ideas to save waste. We introduced a 'no blame' culture – if it doesn't work, no problem, we'll try something else – which took a while to get over. I think it is important that they feel recognised and understand that we are listening.

Taking stock of progress

This culture change programme is characterised by a series of initiatives, all intertwined with Smurfit's MFCI philosophy. Concepts involved include flexible working, self-development, idea generation schemes, continuous training and development, devolved responsibility to first line management and transfer of training responsibility to the line. For a traditional, hierarchical operation, the effect of all of these change initiatives could have become somewhat bewildering.

How do you assess the progress made and the ownership of this new philosophy?

I see a number of examples of 'winners'; the 24 people of the 80 workforce who volunteered for NVQ training; the front line managers who are doing NVQs on supervisory skills, business management and IT skills; the practical ideas generated from the MFCI workshops; the management team's recognition and support of many of the Investors in People principles.

What about the blocks to change you have had to deal with?

There is a hard core, who will never change. People who come in at 8am, leave at 4.30pm and take their pay packets home on Thursdays. These are the few who felt they were unique to the system and didn't have to change.

How did you deal with them?

We talked to them and, if necessary, took disciplinary action. We got the union representatives involved. They helped all of us to see the two sides of the picture, which helped.

So the union representatives were actually committed to playing a constructive role in the change process?

Yes, they did agree that we should go down this road. They were kept informed and involved. They worked with front line managers on how to deal with disciplinary issues. I was aiming to transfer responsibility away from HR to the line.

Against all of this, what now do you see to be the next phase?

The management team will need to begin to think more about our future operations. We need to be sure that we put the right people in the right jobs. We are currently in a state of flux as we move from a manufacturing to a business area responsibility. Much more needs to be done, but the foundations have been laid. Within all of this, my aspiration would be to position HR more in a business planning, as distinct from a personnel services role.

Lessons of a change leader

What, from all of this, have you learnt about change leadership?

From my perspective, the key learning points would be:

- the need to establish open communications with all of the workforce, so they feel involved and an important part of the business
- the importance of establishing trust with the people on the shop floor, the management and the unions

- the need to seed ideas and test the frontiers of thinking when introducing change
- the importance of being pragmatic and practical
- the requirement to have a collaborative relationship with the union reps.
- the potential that people have, at the workforce level, to wish to learn more.

For myself, the whole process has been empowering. Some three years ago I was carrying out a normal personnel administration role. Now I feel stronger not only to facilitate change, but also to challenge things.

The lesson from the Smurfit case is that change need not be a threat, but can become empowering if tackled in terms of personal learning. Over and above this, any change has an inevitable ripple effect which needs to be anticipated and led.

In this case, the ripple effect could be described as:

- a new owner's corporate business philosophy,

leading to:

- a group-wide commitment to managing for continuous improvement (MFCI),

responded to by local management through:

- the introduction of an Investors in People programme, coupled with NVQs,

resulting in:

- 30 per cent of the workforce committing themselves to personal development through NVQs,

requiring:

- a management response on future job roles and opportunities, and hence demanding:

- a clear view on future business strategy, leadership approach, organisation structure, roles and responsibilities.

Against our model on change leadership competencies

It is interesting to stand back from this case and consider the competencies that Phylis McKain and her management team have demonstrated.

Change visionary competencies

The vision is that of the Smurfit Group and their commitment to a managing for continuous improvement philosophy. The translation of this for the Whitehaven Factory was to focus on quality, flexible working and Investors in People.

– the 'shaping the way forward' competencies.

Change influencer competencies

The influencing approach which emerges is that of Phylis taking on personal responsibility as a 'change champion'. The focus which emerges is based on open communication, involvement, education, personal development and pragmatism – an empowering, as distinct from challenging positioning. The concept of an 'idea-seeder' also emerges, who 'tests the frontiers' of what management will accept.

– the competencies of 'building organisation commitment and ownership'.

In terms of the challenge process, the key lever is about meeting the Investors in People criteria. The original case-study illustrated the gaps between historical practice and future requirements; the concept of 'lip service' emerges. In the next phase

Phylis perceives herself as needing to become a part of the planning process and be more ready to challenge.

– the willingness to stand apart and challenge competencies.

The change facilitator competencies

This case is predominantly one of change facilitation. The communication to and involvement of people, the MFCI workshops and idea generation, and the investment in people development to broaden outlooks, are all underpinned by a basic set of values around the willingness of people to respond positively to change.

– the stimulation of innovation competencies.

Trust, pragmatism and doggedness are all essential parts of the change process. Trust requires openness, regular communication, mutual respect and a willingness to see issues from both sides. The constructive role of the unions is a reinforcement of this approach.

– the capacity to be open-minded to others' views and needs competencies.

The Smurfit case gives many insights into the practical consequences of group-wide policies on traditional, regional factories. For companies acquiring others, there appears to be a key challenge to ensure that a coherent strategy for integration is developed, which incorporates considerations of culture and attitude change.

Our thanks are due to the Smurfit Composites management team in Cumbria for allowing us to learn from their experience. Particularly, we thank Phylis McKain for sharing her story of personal discovery, which moves from feeling 'terrified' to facing the next phase 'empowered and confident to challenge'.

13

A Portfolio of Change Agendas

In this chapter we seek to demonstrate the breadth of the change agenda that HR can face. The portfolio encompasses:

- Allied–Distillers – where the business focus is the rationalisation of their traditional distillery operations and the need to develop a partnership between the line and employees to face change together
- Quicks Group – where the business focus is to position people and culture as central to the planned growth of a leading retailing distributor
- Courage Breweries – where the business focus is rapid growth in Europe, underpinned by a realignment of the leadership competencies required and the HR role, and with many of the traditional HR transferred back to the line
- Do-It-All – where the business focus is to respond to a declining market situation in the DIY sector through the introduction of management coaching and mentoring
- Grattans – where the business focus through a major recession has had to be sustaining performance. This case vividly illustrates the changing leadership styles required to move from defending performance to planning for growth.

Case-study: Allied–Distillers

Responding to a declining market by developing a partnership between the line and employees to face change together

Allied–Distillers is the whisky distilling arm of the Allied Domecq spirits and wine business. The whisky business is one very much dominated by the original family-based local community distillery – a sound concept when business growth is guaranteed; however, very much at risk if markets decline across a whole business sector.

Allied–Distillers was the source of around 20 per cent of Allied Domecq's profits, and therefore a crucial business. It has always considered itself very successful; it has had major investment and considers itself technically sophisticated. However, recent changes in the economic and market environments were putting pressure on profits.

In April 1995 John Refaussé was appointed as the first HR director in this 2,000-employee distilling and marketing company. It had been realised that an evolutionary approach to change would not be sufficient: a more radical philosophy was needed.

Threats

World whisky sales were declining in core markets. There was increasing competition and pressure on margins was intense. These realities were included in a major presentation by the managing director to all members of the workforce in April, 1995. This presentation offered a new deal to the workforce based on a recognition of mutual rights and obligations, described as a 'business partnership'.

Internal pressures

The company recognised the need to review its management style and capabilities and radically update working practices and procedures. In addition the business had just been redesignated from a profit-centre to a cost-centre. This in turn increased the pressure for change to operational practices. The operations director, having visited Japan, wanted to develop the concept of 'high performance teams' and launched *Project Star*, which was aimed at creating the environment for teamwork to be fostered.

Blockages to change

The IR environment was highly formalised and inflexible; it was an adversarial, conflict-type situation. The trade unions tended to communicate with employees, but managers rarely communicated directly, other than in formal presentation sessions. Personnel had not previously been represented on the board. The personnel role was a 'traditional' one: that of a company policeman and keeper of the IR rules and procedures.

Facilitating the change

Much of the initial preparation work for the change programme had been pioneered by Kevin Eyre, who was appointed HR development manager approximately 18 months earlier. His prime role was to act as a catalyst for change. Kevin's concept was to develop a partnership between the line and the employees, together to face up to the required agenda for change. The inertia against change was seen as a major issue in an environment where a more radical philosophy was needed. Managers who perceived a need to behave differently began to work with him. An early role model was established through the creation and resourcing of a new logistics function in the business. Kevin had worked with some senior line managers to develop the competencies of work groups, such as their listening skills and communication abilities. Unfortunately, because objectives at this stage were not clear, some managers, employees and trade unions resisted the change process and progress with *Project Star* began to falter.

A new personnel director

As the new personnel director, John Refaussé's major task was the implementation of a 'partnership agreement' that Kevin Eyre had developed. This agreement was constructed so that, in exchange for the abandonment of a range of restrictive practices, management would provide investment in training and development, a commitment to job security, a new incentive scheme, and joint planning for the creation of high-performance work groups.

John's change initiatives were to train managers to negotiate a deal which went well beyond conventional bargaining; to establish a board-level change strategy group; to restructure the HR function (with a series of new appointments and reorganised roles, the function was to reorientate from the traditional control, administration, negotiation function, to change facilitators, supporting a corporate change strategy); and to develop a communication strategy (communication becomes line-, not trade union-driven, and managers are trained in two-way communication). There was also a need to face the operations management team with the challenge of managing changes necessary to establish the company as a centre of manufacturing excellence. In this process it was necessary to identify those managers who would be unable to adapt to a change culture.

The change negotiation

In June, following tough negotiations, the full-time officials of the three unions agreed the deal. The workforce rejected it. The reason for the rejection seemed to be that the workforce did not trust management's ability to manage change sympathetically. John recognised that, to gain trust, management had to exhibit significantly different behaviour.

The change agenda adopted by HR and endorsed by the ADL board was to ensure that line management, not HR, negotiated the deal; line management, not the trade unions, was required to take the lead in communicating with the workforce. Following further discussions, and in spite of strong trade union support, the deal was subsequently rejected a second time, and there was a threat of strike action. However, the climate was beginning to change.

A voluntary redundancy programme had meant that about 200 employees had decided to leave the business. They had largely been those who would have found it hardest to work in the proposed new high-performance team environment. New appointments to senior roles, some from other companies, had been made and these were emerging as a focus for continuing change. HR's role was now recognised as a facilitator of change, rather than a control system that blocked any tendency to change.

A significant step forward on the partnership agreement came in early October with the blue-collar union committing to shed a range of restrictive practices and to work towards a range of common goals aimed at improving efficiency and job security.

Lessons on change leadership

From John Refaussé's standpoint, he had inherited a situation where Kevin Eyre had developed a profound vision of a business partnership, a substantial change from the historical paternalistic autocracy. The resulting inertia and reluctance to change were the problems he faced. The change leadership lessons he drew were:

- the importance of director-level counselling and coaching – the major change required was by the directors themselves; to stay with the traditional style of leadership would have maintained the *status quo*. The challenge was to develop a new style of leadership more in line with the need to think strategically and respond to market change with greater urgency.
- the need to address directly the perceived blocks to change – against the HR intention of creating business partnerships, the weight of history, and the inevitable inertia against change, this was somewhat submerged. To achieve the new vision the cultural inertia needed to be addressed.
- the requirement to take a longer-term perspective cannot avoid business reality – the transition from traditional, pater-nalistic leadership to that of co-operative partnerships in

future change was substantial and as such required a long-haul perspective. However, business reality required more radical and drastic action in terms of changing working practices, downsizing and business restructuring.

- the need for HR to assume a more proactive and assertive role – the paternalistic style was somewhat reassuring and welcoming. For HR, the comfort generated somewhat clouded the need for an urgent, proactive and assertive challenge.

Against our model of change leadership

The change visionary competencies

Kevin Eyre's vision of building co-operative partnerships on future change was fundamental.

– the shaping competencies.

His initial diagnosis was sound about the need for the business to adapt and respond to market change together. The inertia of history demonstrated that this had not been part of the traditional paternalistic culture.

– the scanning and interrogating competencies.

The change influencing competencies

Change influencing was very much positioned around the role of the MD and the top team. The HR philosophy and approach was one of empowerment as distinct from direct intervention.

–the organisation-influencing competencies.

Kevin Eyre's initial diagnosis would have prepared the organisation to face up to future challenges. However, the required culture change process proved to be too prolonged in the face of ever-pressing business reality. Renegotiation with the unions on working practices proved to be a key starting position.

— the standing apart and challenging competencies.

The change facilitator competencies

The change process is predominantly one of change facilitation: a process of building, as distinct from a challenging philosophy. Success was to be determined by a change in director-level behaviour and attitudes. As such, a line-directed change programme was envisaged.

— the open-minded competencies.

The emphasis on MD and director-level coaching sought to empower them to lead change.

— the empathising competencies.

Case-study: Quicks Group plc

Breaking out and building for the future through people

Quicks Group is the 15th largest retailer of motor vehicles and vehicle parts in the UK. It operates from 30 locations across the UK and holds 10 manufacturers' franchises. There are a total of 1,500 employees.

In 1991 Alec Murray joined as chief executive after almost 30 years worldwide with Ford, emerging finally as managing director of Ford Credit Europe. When Alex Murray arrived, he was faced with a business which had in 1991 a loss of £1,000,000. In contrast, in 1994 Quicks made a £3.9 million profit.

He outlined his vision of this business as:

> To be acknowledged by customers, suppliers, employees and shareholders as the best retailer of automotive products in the UK.

> In pursuit of this mission, the group will encourage, involve, train and develop its people to continuously improve their skills, to the mutual benefit of customers, shareholders and employees.

In 1992 a new group personnel manager, Eve Beresford, was appointed. She brought to the post a professional training, via IPD examination, together with experience of HR in other major businesses, in contrast to her predecessor who was an ex-line manager who retired after holding the post for 18 years. During this time the department had provided a largely reactive support to line management. A considerable amount of its time was spent responding to employment regulatory-type matters, such as dismissal and redundancies.

In addition to Eve, the HR department now has one other qualified professional and a student on secondment from university.

In the period ahead Alec Murray sees the need to plan for considerable change. The changes involve investment in premises and technology, in expansion of the group and the development and recruitment of skilled staff.

HR was thus provided with an opportunity to influence in a 'warm climate' with substantial support from the chief executive, which was vital to the success of the change initiatives which were to follow. However, because of the limited HR budget, it had to achieve it in a very cost-effective manner.

HR's initiatives

To establish itself as a net contributor to the business, the prime HR initiative was to seek to realign the department from a largely reactive role to that of a strategic partner with a focus on creating an environment that was conducive to change.

Recognising that people were somewhat bruised by the extent of the change that had taken place over the preceding years, in order to be successful the approach had to recognise that people felt insecure and apprehensive. Therefore any conventional approach such as 'top-down' would have driven the negative response further, while 'bottom-up' change was asking a great deal of people who were insecure.

The approach that was used incorporated elements from many well-known methods which were familiar to both Alec Murray and Eve, eg, empowerment, re-engineering, the power of learning. A variety of HR projects have been used as change agents. The main feature of these new, tightly-linked HR processes is to establish partnerships at all levels throughout the company. Change has therefore taken place by respecting the existing values and norms and using them to drive the culture forward to an acceptance of new behaviours and beliefs.

Dismissal initiatives

In 1992 the company lost about £150,000 in tribunal and associated costs, mainly because managers had little understanding of employment law and how to operate the company disciplinary procedures. Line managers tended to act without reference to HR, which they involved only after an individual had been told they were to be dismissed. Eve Beresford spent six months 'educating' managers to change their approach to dismissals and to involve her whenever they were contemplating disciplinary action.

Given that the sites were geographically dispersed and that the managers had little knowledge of what were 'reasonable' actions, she spent the initial months on the telephone providing advice. She changed the perception of HR by providing advice and coaching but not carrying out the dismissals.

When the managers had gained a reasonable level of competence and confidence, and recognising that to continue this 'firefighting and education' approach was a considerable constraint on any other initiatives, and having no other staff, the next stage was to outsource the responsibility to a lawyer specialising in employment law. Having achieved this, Eve then used the time to identify an external supplier of computer services who would work with her to design a user-friendly program which would act as a guide through the disciplinary process and provide standardised documentation which met all statutory requirements. In addition, the system was designed to provide a monitoring facility and management controls. The system has been successfully tested for six months in one-third of the company and will shortly be rolled out to the remainder of the company.

The success of the system is due not only to its design but also largely because of the partnerships built with the people who are responsible for the system in each location. The people selected to be trained have been so successful they are now working towards the Certificate in Personnel Practice. When they have gained this qualification they will be regraded and change their job title to personnel administrator.

Beginning to devolve personnel administration closer to the line has provided line managers with 'on the spot' personnel support, while enhancing the status of those involved with the department. This MIS process and Eve's manager education programme has reduced the tribunal cost to £10,000. Managerial involvement at tribunal stage is now minimal; directors are now rarely involved.

Line managers' perception is beginning to change; they now understand that central HR is moving from an administrative, reactive function to one which provides 'sound' advice, and saves money and line managers' time. Also, as managers operate the correct disciplinary procedure, a change in management style is becoming apparent throughout the company.

Staff competencies

Eve recognised that if Quicks were to be able to meet the vision of a continuous skills development business, she had to have a process that would achieve this. An initial review of the applications for trainee positions in the group showed that:

- most of the applicants were male
- applicants perceived Quicks as having only technical jobs
- schools, careers advisers and parents all considered that the company had no jobs other than technical.

She therefore considered that if Quicks were to attract better-quality staff, it would be necessary to:

- develop a career structure that would attract and motivate different types of recruits
- develop a training/education process which would change the skill, knowledge and attitude base of new staff.

Blocks to change

Internal

- Line managers had little or no experience of other than technical training. Their only experience of training was to allow the trainee to attend college on day release.
- They generally adopted a style which tended to work around 'central' staff initiatives.
- They usually concerned themselves only with initiatives that had relatively quick 'bottom line' results.
- They were normally resistant to change.

External

- It was necessary to change the perception of Quicks within the education establishment and the community in general.

Competence initiative

In order to meet the vision and overcome the blocks to change, Eve initiated the *Quickstart Experience*, which is a 25-hour project involving local schools. It gives local pupils the opportunity to see how technology is used within Quicks. They have first-hand experience of all business departments. The programme is benchmarked against elements of NVQs and is endorsed by the City of Salford Education Department and Manchester TEC. The *Quickstart Experience* has now run for two years and has begun to change the perceptions of the education establishment and parents towards careers in Quicks.

The next part of this initiative is the *Extended Placements* scheme. This was researched, designed and implemented by HR as a pilot system of extended placements, taking children from local schools and inviting them to spend half a day every week within a Quicks dealership for up to one school year. This gave pupils the opportunity to learn about Quicks and to experience the job they thought they would like to do when they left school. During the time they spend with Quicks, they work towards obtaining units in the relevant occupational areas they wish to explore. Managers are taking a keen interest in the scheme and are becoming involved in providing learning opportunities for the school pupils.

The figures below indicate the 1996 applications for the *Extended Placements*: the quality and attitude of these people is considerably higher than is usual with new recruits.

NVQ training

Technical	Whole-saling	Finance	Sales	Customer service	Adminis-tration
49	16	4	5	5	19

The effects of the initiatives

HR has become more proactive; it no longer acts in a firefighting manner. Line managers now request advice and assistance before they act in employment law-type matters. The *Quickstart Experience* has resulted in general managers asking for placement students as a means of recruiting, recognising that this will reduce labour turnover and provide them with a steady source of trainees who have already proved their value. Those managers who have embraced the initiatives more completely are experiencing 'bottom line' improvements. The organisation is beginning to differentiate between personnel administration, which now takes place in the business units, and the strategic HR which takes place centrally.

HR's reflection on its change leadership style

Within an organisational climate where the dominant management style was authoritative, it would have been difficult, if not impossible, to achieve change in a tough-minded influencer manner. Change has taken place via the capacity of HR to link its own initiatives with the MD's vision and to facilitate change through its capacity to coach and counsel line managers and to show that its initiatives are consistent with those of line managers (mainly the general managers of the business units); that is, they positively contribute to trading success.

Further HR changes are likely to follow this model of seeking to understand the strategic imperatives and then ensure that HR processes are supportive of them. The HR approach is likely to be a partnership with the line, rather than imposed from the top, so that they not only endorse the changes but are motivated because the changes enhance the individual GM's success, the sites' success and ultimately the MD's and the business's success. This means that a major competency for HR management is to be recognised as a business partner with HR competencies, rather than someone who takes 'HR initiatives'.

However, the overriding key to the success of the change programme has been the ability to understand the main drivers of the culture accurately and work with, rather than across, them. It is here that the approach to change has been genuinely

different. The construction of this approach was a blend of Alec
Murray's extensive experience of a variety of change management processes over a 30-year period with a large multi-national,
and Eve's ability to harmonise her knowledge and understanding
of strategic HR to change the existing culture in a focused and
integrative style.

Against our model of change leadership

The change visionary competencies

The new CEO, from outside the motor trade, clearly articulated
his vision for the future of Quicks with an emphasis on people
and culture change.

— the shaping competencies.

Within the mission statement, the CEO clearly recognised that
customer service and retention through motivated and involved
staff would deliver a distinctive competitive advantage in a
sector dominated by task and mechanical skills.

— the scanning and interrogating competencies.

The change influencing competencies

The influencing approach adopted by HR as a 'problem remover
and counsellor' reflected the strong bottom-line cultural history.
A non-interventionist posture was taken in working with the line
on their business agenda.

— the organisation-influencing competencies.

The new CEO had the vision and courage to challenge the
historical management style and practices. The next phase for
HR, having established initial credibility, would be to work in

partnership with the CEO to lead the culture change process required.

> – *the standing apart and challenging competencies.*

The change facilitator competencies

The case is demonstrably one where HR has decided on a facilitating role. The cost of tribunals and the line management time involved created the 'pain' which needed to be cured. The HR response of advising and educating on good practices to deal with the causes rather than the symptoms proved to be a dose of preventive medicine, which was welcomed.

> – *the empathising and empowering competencies.*

The initiatives on changing the employment market's image of Quicks demonstrated a high degree of innovative HR. The *Quickstart Experience* is a vivid example here.

> – *the innovation competencies.*

Case-study: Courage Breweries

Planning for business growth through new leadership competencies and a changed role of HR

Courage is a brewing company with 4,665 employees (in 1995). The industry tends to consider itself to be a traditional one.

Colin Ions is now HR director of Courage, and has been with Courage for 18 years. His case-study shows how HR's influence is dependent on the degree to which its initiatives are supportive of the business strategy. In 1989 he was HR manager, and with his then director sought to provide initiatives for the brewing business that would change a traditional industry significantly.

Corporate vision

The CEO had defined his vision of becoming a European business – and one that needed to double its market share. To achieve these changes, HR recognised that there had to be major changes in the competency profiles of the management. It also recognised that HR had to be refocused.

HR initiatives

To enable management to lead the change successfully, a change management workshop programme was designed. These programmes were provided for all senior managers, and later for all staff. They were provided in-house and had a significant project basis; that is, having learned how to lead change, managers were required to undertake a change exercise.

These change programmes not only improved the skills of managers and staff, they also revealed that some managers were not able to develop the required competencies. This led to further HR initiatives: a programme to eliminate the change blockers, and using those who were highly competent change leaders to unblock some change initiatives or enhance others.

The change leader style of HR

HR was thus acting as a change influencer, having had the capacity to envision a change initiative which supported the business goals. They were challenging performances assertively and manpower-planning proactively to ensure that those who were competent change leaders were located in roles where their style met the business needs.

To be able to influence senior managers to support the change workshops, accept staff reduction and staff relocation, HR changed its own role, function and style. HR influence was significantly enhanced by its willingness to act as a role model.

Following the merging of Courage and Grand Metropolitan's brewing interests, HR reduced its headcount from 198 in 1991 to

58 in 1995. The HR budget was reduced from £11m to £6.5m. As a function, its reductions were greater than any other.

The role performed by HR changed from being a supplier of HR services to the line, to consultancy to line. HR skills such as recruitment, performance management, employment law and IR negotiation were transferred to line. The role of HR director was transformed from one which had power because of its technical knowledge to one which had influence because it could facilitate change.

Fellow directors and senior managers are now less likely to ask HR for technical advice than they are to seek guidance on how they might more effectively work with other managers or teams. It would appear that HR has, by reducing the demands from line management for technical information and tactical response, been able to make the time for strategic vision, and thereby be able to develop a partnership role with the CEO, and a facilitator role with senior colleagues. However, without the tough-minded approach to the management of HR, it would have been unlikely that the function would have had the respect and thereby the influence on line managers.

The continuing influence of HR will be a function of its customer satisfaction; Colin Ions therefore initiated a customer-satisfaction survey for HR. Perceiving HR as a service and being willing, in a tough-minded way, to test customer reaction to the service (like the willingness to 'steal financial management's clothes' by taking a tougher budget line than they), gives HR the ability to role-model and influence through example. Traditional management had been influenced to change through training, coaching and counselling. Where resistance to change was the norm, rapid adaptation has become the valued competency.

Lessons on change leadership

Perhaps Courage had the courage to let go of tradition. As André Gide said when commenting on courage:

one doesn't discover new lands without consenting to lose
sight of the shore for a very long time.

Courage had to let go of tried and tested theories to be able to
work successfully with Grand Metropolitan. At least one of their
navigators was HR which had the bravery to let go of its
traditional role.

Against our model of change leadership

The change visionary competencies

The vision articulated was that of the CEO with an emphasis on
creating a European business with rapid market growth. For HR,
their vision was that to achieve this, new leadership and managerial competencies would be required.

– the shaping competencies.

The recognition that a change in leadership style was needed to
face the future was fundamental; a traditional style of management would have been too ponderous and slow to react.

– the scanning and interrogating competencies.

The change visionary competencies

The most dramatic aspect of the case is the decision by HR to
change its role by transferring HR responsibilities back to the
line and assuming a more change coaching style. This required
both courage and vision on Colin Ions' part.

– the willingness to stand apart and challenge.

The approach to organisation-influencing was to position HR as
a role model. To challenge performance, to develop change

leader competencies and to re-allocate strength to key roles was a tough-minded and necessary stance.

> – *the assertiveness competencies.*

The change facilitation competencies

The introduction of change leadership and management work-shops aimed to empower managers to respond to change. This, coupled with the coaching role adopted by HR, served to enable change to be led by the line.

> – *the empathising competencies.*

The change workshops enabled managers to consider their response to the blocks to change. The emphasis on 'rapid adaptation' has thrown down the gauntlet for improvement and responsiveness.

> – *the innovative competencies.*

Case-study: Do-It-All

Developing a coaching style of management

Do-It-All was jointly owned by Boots and WH Smith until July 1996 when WH Smith sold its 50 per cent share to Boots. It has 199 stores and 5,000 employees. Nic Turner is organisational development manager, responsible to Geoff Kidd the personnel director. He has been with Do-It-All for two-and-a-half years.

The board of Do-It-All, advised by consultants, decided that as a relatively small player in a diminishing market (from 1991 onwards the housing market had shrunk significantly) they had to differentiate themselves from the competition. The way they chose to do this was through the projection of a powerful brand image. The quality of customer service was seen to be one of the most important elements in the delivery of a differentiated brand.

Personnel initiative

Geoff Kidd recognised that the merger and its associated delayering and store closures, and the downturn in the market, had created a defensive culture. The executive board identified the need, if a customer services orientation was to be achieved, to create a culture where trust and confidence in management was re-established. An organisation development manager was appointed to act as a catalyst for this cultural change.

Observing the management style and its associated practices and processes, Nic Turner identified a command-and-control climate where initiative, risk and innovation were not encouraged and individual learning outside the management-determined 'answers' was very limited. To achieve the change from a situation where an operative, if instructed to fill a shelf would do so and would continue to follow that instruction whatever happened around him, to one where an operative filling a shelf would continually seek opportunities to help colleagues and customers, Nic recognised he had to produce a large-scale culture change.

Nic's vision was that the change process had to have a rapid impact across the organisation, and be able to change the paradigm by which staff at all levels understood themselves and their effectiveness. A five-stage change programme was designed:

- Stage one was the introduction of an upward appraisal system for all managers.
- Stage two was a two-and-a-half-day programme designed to help managers to change their self- and interpersonal-

understanding and behaviour. Using the concept of the 'inner game of tennis' and using tennis as a training process, Nic's programme – beginning with the board – enabled staff more fully to understand their own and others' feelings and thoughts, such that their interactions changed from being instruction-led to being customer, co-worker and self-led.

- The third stage was the development of 'co-coaching and/or facilitation by personnel'. It should be noted that personnel had attended a two-and-a-half-day programme that provided considerable coaching and facilitation training to enable them to change their thoughts and behaviour from their self-image as part of the company's control systems, to that of facilitators to line management.
- The fourth stage (six months later) was a review of how managers had put the programme into effect.
- The fifth stage was a repeat of the upward appraisal and a report to the board on the management style of the business.

Concurrent with all these stages Nic was increasing his influence through his coaching and facilitation of senior staff and work teams. He estimates that in 1993 he spent 10 per cent of his time as a personal coach and facilitator of work groups; he estimates that he now spends 80 per cent of his time in these roles.

Developing skills and teamwork within the personnel function

Nic joined a relatively traditional personnel function, split between those people involved in personnel work and those involved in training. The culture change programme and the skills development necessary to deliver it gave these two groups a common purpose and a shared learning experience. A skilled, committed and unified team evolved to deliver the programme and to support its transference into the business. Without this team the work would not have been possible.

The change leader style of personnel

Nic's style was initially visionary. He had, for his three-month induction period, to be able to remain open to the external ideas of those he observed, and to the ideas he had brought from his intellectual and life experiences: from NLP (Neuro Linguistic Programming) to Indians (North American and sub-continental), from counselling theory to Zen. He had to have the courage and influencing skills to challenge the MD and the executive board. He needed the facilitation skills to be psychologically-minded, to help managers understand their feelings about the changes and to help them understand how they could learn and change. He needed to inspire, train and develop a team, over which he had no formal authority, to do the work.

Overview

Two years on, the results of the changes appear, from managers' comments, to be improved staff morale, decreased absenteeism, and more effective teamwork. The cumulative data on the management style of the organisation shows significant improvement (more than 25 per cent) in:

- effectiveness of meetings
- questioning skills
- performance feedback
- inspirational leadership
- flexibility of view
- people development
- creating ownership and responsibility
- creating enthusiasm and loyalty
- processing, encouraging and developing team spirit.

Managers report that they find their work more enjoyable as the trust in their individuals and teams is repaid in improved performance. The management effectiveness of the business, on the basis of the upward appraisal, has improved by a third in the last year. Additionally, managers in transition – for example, those forming a new work-team – now request personnel to act as facilitators. An example of the change is that Nic was asked to facilitate the organisation's sales and marketing meeting. He has now been asked to chair it.

Personnel's role has changed from being that of the company policeman (part of the command-and-control system), to the facilitators of change, working with managers on their decisions, communications and other processes. They are now an integral part of the management processes, but they have the additional virtue that they are able to adopt an 'independent' perspective.

Personnel staff now work with 'real' teams on major business issues. A new team will request personnel to facilitate their review of how they operate, what tasks they should undertake, who should do the tasks, and what their strategy should be. Perhaps Nic's experiences, and his on-going commitment to his own personal and intellectual growth, have ensured that he had belief in himself and thereby could facilitate organisation change.

Against our model of change leadership

The change visionary competencies

The diagnosis by Geoff Kidd, further reinforced by Nic Turner, was that in a diminishing market place Do-It-All needed to reposition itself as a niche player and hence differentiate its brand from competitors by a high customer-service reputation.

– the shaping competencies.

The essential part of the diagnosis was that the do-it-yourself market was determined by the strength of the economy and of the housing market. Customer service, control of stock costs, productivity and performance, the impact of technology, all had a major impact on survival.

> – *the scanning and interrogating competencies.*

The change influencing competencies

Initially, Geoff Kidd and later Nic Turner had the courage to challenge the impact of store closure and organisation delayering on the creation of a defensive culture. These insights were key to the shift away from 'command-and-control' to a 'coaching' style of management. The upward appraisal system further reinforced this challenge.

> – *the standing apart competencies.*

The toughest challenge was to the line itself, to reconsider its style and impact. The shift to a coaching style of management was induced by the regular upward appraisal process. The positioning of HR as a role model further demonstrated this thrust.

> – *the organisation influencing competencies.*

The change facilitator competencies

The commitment to coaching is the dominant message from this case. This, coupled with the training in self-knowledge and interpersonal sensitivity, aimed to empower the line manager and enable them to self-develop and adapt.

> – *the empowerment and empathising competencies.*

The emphasis on self-management and development, coupled with regular upward feedback and on-going coaching, was aimed at encouraging managers to resolve their own change leadership agendas both for themselves and their teams. The commitment to culture change and the encouragement of staff to be continuous improvers was also evident.

> – *the open-minded competencies.*

Case-study: Grattan plc

Rebuilding business performance through changing the leadership style

A history of changing ownership

Grattan plc is a leading UK mail-order company based in Bradford. As with all companies in the retail sector, during the 1991 to 1994 recession the company had been striving to sustain business performance and margins. Many tough decisions have had to be made to protect profitability and turn around performance.

In order survive, top management has had to take a 'hard line' on business costs and management performance:

- staffing levels reduced from 4,250 to 3,500
- renegotiation of critical union agreements to move from guaranteed to performance-related earnings
- introduction of new senior and middle management talent; some 40 per cent of the top 75 were changed.

Over and above this, Grattan has experienced a series of 'new dawns' where new owners came in and raised more optimistic expectations for the future:

- Next acquired Grattan in 1986; they set about investing in new technology, both in terms of business control and also the order handling and warehousing processes. Unfortunately this investment ran parallel to a major recession in the UK retail

market and required the 'hard line' decisions made by top
management.

- In 1991 Grattan was sold to Otto Versoud, the leading
  international German mail order company; their ambition was
  to acquire an entry position into the UK market.

This process of tough change had created a battle weariness
within the management structure. There was, in HR terms, a
need to rebuild confidence and new incentives to face up to the
future.

The HR strategy on change

This case-study is presented from two HR standpoints: those of
Norman Finnegan, Operations Director and HR Director, who
had a key role to play in leading and facilitating the process of
'hard decisions' on people and the renegotiation of union
agreements, and more recently to facilitate the top team's
consideration of business mission and strategy; and Julie Sutton,
training and development manager, whose challenge was to
initiate a training programme to re-empower and skill the
organisation to face the challenge of on-going change.

This two-tier approach was important in ensuring that management competencies and the underlying culture were in place
to deliver the Grattan mission 'to be the preferred choice in
home shopping'.

The management development strategy

Phase I: Laying the foundations (1992–93)

The initial diagnosis carried out by Julie and her management
training team indicated a need to build management confidence
and understanding and to engender a belief in their future role
and influence; an aim to lay the foundations for a major culture

change strategy which would enable management at all levels to play their part in rebuilding business performance.

The envisaged cultural shift emphasised:

- the importance of change and adaptation to future success
- team and cross-team working
- individual managers as change influencers, not reactors
- a coaching style of management
- self-development and learning
- a proactive and positive climate for change
- openness, feedback and challenge
- devolution of responsibilities.

A training programme was launched which targeted the senior and middle management levels as both the key opinion formers and the potential initiators of future change.

A workshop programme was developed around:

- 'the management of change'
- 'influencing skills and strategies'
- 'core management skills'.

The workshop concept emphasised dealing with real issues and undertaking 'back at work' project applications, a process which management warmed to and which resulted in a whole array of initiatives and challenge to the *status quo*.

As hoped, a 'middle-up' demand for clarity of business direction emerged, coupled with an increased readiness of management to take responsibility for initiatives at their level.

Phase II: Reviewing progress (July 1993)

The training team was becoming increasingly aware of this upsurge in demand and constructive energy. They sought and

gained Norman Finnegan's support for a management development strategy review to be presented to the top team.

This review, guided by ourselves, sought to address the fit
between the overall business aims and the management development strategy; a review process which would ensure that the
culture change strategy would be formally aligned with business
strategy and leadership. The shift in culture which was emerging
is displayed in Table 3.

Table 3 *Culture shift*

Historical	Current
• a hierarchical directive style	• directors reviewing own leadership impact
• functionalised	• cross-functional networking
• insular, introspective	• change and culture understood
• 'punch drunk' with change	• task forces on key business change issues
• disempowered	• readiness to assume greater responsibility
• piecemeal management competencies	• a trained cadre of management

The training team had now succeeded in positioning themselves
as not only educators but also as change counsellors to interested
directors and managers. As with any culture change initiative,
pockets of success were beginning to emerge, although a total
shift had not yet been achieved.

Over and above this, the review team was determined to
demonstrate a clear link between culture and overall business
performance. The framework in Table 4 proved most insightful
here.

This vision of the business fit and value was a key output of
the review. However, blocks to further progress had to be
confronted, including:

• a directive, top-down management style
• risk aversion and high dependency

- short-term thinking
- top team still 'fire-fighting'
- no shared understanding of business strategy
- gaps in stock of management talent
- issue-based rather than goal-orientated management.

Table 4 *Culture, business fit and performance*

Critical business success factors	Cultural characteristics
• market/business knowledge	• sharing of business issues and priorities
• innovation in customer catalogues	• customer knowledge/focus
• supply-chain management	• cross-team working internally and with suppliers
• product quality reputation	• customer service
• responsiveness to market change	• a proactive climate for change
• external market image	• management behaviour
• productivity/efficiency	• goal and continuous improvement orientation

Phase III: Establishing the business fit

The output of the review was shared with Norman Finnegan; the review team and he judged that an honest and open feedback to the top team would be both timely and constructive.

The options on the way forward to be presented were:

- an organisation-wide culture change programme led by top management
- an opportunistic approach around the reorganisation of marketing, merchandising/stock control and computing
- a top team sponsored series of cross-functional task forces on key business issues.

HR decided to position itself as a challenging, yet pragmatic, change partner. This judgement was based on the initiatives that the top team already had under way in establishing a clear view of corporate mission and values. The emphasis was to be on business fit and focus.

The top team strategy

At the top team level there was a growing recognition of the need to break out of the cycle of focusing on cost control and strong management directives if the intention was to plan for growth. The top team was beginning to recognise that its own leadership style and philosophy could be perceived as a major block to business 'break out'.

The top team had been made aware of, and welcomed, the groundswell of challenge from senior and middle management, many of whom were new. The commitment that Norman had gained for a substantial intake of a new talent, plus the quality of the recruitment process, laid the foundations for this.

The presentation of the management development strategy review served to highlight further the shifts required in leadership style and culture. From the review, which was seen as insightful and, in the main, in line with their emerging views, they determined two courses of action:

- to seek more direct feedback on their leadership style and impact
- to work on the development of statement of business mission, goals and values.

Leadership style and impact

The top team launched a survey which was carried out among the top 24 senior managers, to seek feedback on the key leadership issues of directors' leadership style, the quality of cross-director relationships, the overall management approach, and its effectiveness. The feedback was presented to the top team as part of an offsite teamworking workshop, which sought to develop openness and trust.

The open challenge to leadership effectiveness encouraged the top team to launch a mission and values debate with senior management. The top team's commitment to open leadership was to become a key role model for the rest of the organisation.

Developing business mission and values

A series of top team workshops was carried out in the period through to August 1993 to address corporate mission and values. These were shared and tested with a group of eight senior staff for comment.

The mission and values statement was to be underpinned by a core set of values of 'trust, integrity, communication and empowerment'. These values indicated the strong commitment to culture change which was the key emphasis in the 1992 launch of the new management development strategy. This was achieved through a series of regular discussions between the newly appointed MD and the HR team.

Reviewing the key business process

Over and above the initial consultation with key senior staff, four working groups were established, made up of six senior cross-functional staff, to review the core process and organisational goals in 'customers', 'product offer', 'selling vehicle' and 'service offer'. These were under the direct sponsorship of individual directors. This initiative resulted in some 153 recommendations for improvement in goal achievement. The journey to devolution had begun.

A 'values in action' programme

The training team then set about preparing a framework for reviewing the newly-defined values in action. This sought to address the key shortfalls in any 'mission and values' exercise of the risk of statements with no real measurables.

A team review workbook was designed which took each value and linked it to a practical leadership action, as shown below.

Value	Leadership practice
TRUST	• to develop on-going trusting relationship with colleagues
	• to ensure quality internal customer relationships
	• to encourage cross-team collaboration
	• to encourage staff to be open with feelings and thoughts
	• to be open and direct in communications

These practices were enlarged upon with a measurable set of actions and success criteria.

The plan was to launch the need for these team reviews across the whole organisation through a series of cross-functional seminars, starting initially with the top 24 and then covering the whole of the organisation.

This was a highly visible campaign which aimed to ensure that everyone accepted the organisation's values and the changes needed in their own behaviour and practices.

Lessons on change leadership

These are presented from the standpoints of Norman Finnegan, the HR and operations director, and Julie Sutton, the training and development manager. Interestingly, during the period described Norman's own role changed to incorporate the responsibilities of the operations director. This meant he had direct responsibility for 2,800 of the total 4,000 staff; a unique position which meant he could both facilitate, implement and influence change directly.

The programme of management team reviews has succeeded in developing a whole series of improvement initiatives. Over and above this, it has demonstrated management's willingness to be open and challenging, a key step on the road to culture change. Plans are now being made to extend the process into the supervisory and operational levels.

From the personnel director's viewpoint the key lessons were:

- the importance of 'sanity checks' whereby top team level initiatives are tested out with a cross-section of senior management who would be responsible for their implementation, eg the mission and values statements.
- the need to accept that culture change is a long-term, as distinct from short-term, process. Within this, the recruitment of quality players at the senior and middle management levels has a key part to play in shaping a future vision of the business: it created a more proactive rather than reactive potential.
- the key requirement to ensure that within a dynamic environment Grattan needs to be the first to spot an opportunity and seize it; a shift which would require a higher level of initiative-taking throughout the whole organisation. He also identifies that it will take considerable effort to spread the new culture throughout the whole organisation. However, in this the personnel function has a key part to play as a role model, in being open, trusting, challenging and empowering.
- the potential in a philosophy of empowerment which will enable the top team to focus on the longer term, while delegating responsibility for operational matters to senior management. For a top team which has had to live through an era of short-term tough decisions, this commitment is essential to the culture change strategy envisaged. To move from 'hands-on' towards 'strategic leadership' was the key leadership determination.
- the need to ensure that all 4,000 employees feel customer-focused, empowered and in a learning environment where the

individual and teamwork are valued. The top team is already
there, management is moving in this direction, and the workforce is the next change-leadership challenge. The focus for
the future will inevitably be on the supervisors and their
natural work teams.

In terms of the training and development manager's perspective
the lessons were:

- the importance of individuals believing in their own power
  and influence. The tough line required in the early days meant
  that managers were forced into a reactive role. In the future
  they will need to take more initiative at their level.
- the benefit to be gained in providing 'back at work' counsel
  and support. On-going confidence- and skill-building were
  essential planks in creating the new culture.
- the value in opportunism, to move forward with interested
  directors, rather than seeking total organisational change; to
  follow a pragmatic, as distinct from idealistic, approach to
  change leadership.
- the importance of 'business fit'. Management development
  and culture change can appear to be a soft option, focusing on
  the needs of people. The key shift achieved in the overall
  strategy was to link the management development and business strategies.

Against our model of change leadership

The change visionary competencies

The emphasis in the early phase of the Grattan change programme was on facilitation. The management development
review was key to raising the need for business fit and direction.
This resulted in the business mission and values exercise.

  – the shaping of the future competencies.

The emphasis placed on culture change, and on the link with the business-critical success factors, raised training on to the business agenda. The current commitment to expand the new culture throughout the organisation is seen to be key to responding to opportunities quicker than the competition. New skills and processes will be required here.

> *– the scanning of the environment competencies.*

The change influencing competencies

Norman's role in dealing with the tough decisions on manning levels, quality of management, and trade union agreements all set the tone for the future. The influencing strategy used to win support of these changes was crucial.

> *– the organisation influencing competencies.*

The management development review and the open and honest feedback to the top team reinforced the need to look at their leadership.

> *– the standing apart competencies.*

The change facilitator competencies

The case-study presented is predominantly one of facilitating change. The testing of the mission and values with representative senior management demonstrated a willingness to be open and to share thinking. The positive response to the 'middle-up' groundswell also demonstrated an open leadership philosophy.

> *– the open-minded competencies.*

The task forces which generated some 153 ideas vividly demonstrated the benefits in participation and devolution.

> *– the idea generation competencies.*

Our thanks are due to Norman Finnegan and Julie Sutton for allowing us to learn from their experience. The case presented is an insightful demonstration of the people and culture change factors involved in moving from a necessarily tough, hands-on regime to one of devolved and shared responsibilities.

14

▚ Practical Change Leadership Strategies

An overview of insights from the case-studies

By including case-studies in this book, our aim was to learn from practical, real-life experience. We were determined to adopt a listening and learning stance. In doing this, we sought to learn from practice and then develop our concepts on successful change leadership and influencing strategies; a bias which sought to emphasise the pragmatic and, perhaps, realistic approach as distinct from a theoretical prescription.

On analysing the case-studies, which embrace a whole spectrum of businesses operating in different market sectors, with major differences in size and complexity, it is surprising to see the amount of common ground emerging from successful change strategies.

The following pages describe the key areas requiring consideration when planning a major change initiative.

The need for a clear business rationale and change leadership philosophy

In this current era of rapid and accelerating change, managers and employees are inevitably increasingly suspicious and mistrustful of change. Frequent reorganisations, downsizing, business process re-engineering, and being persuaded of the substantial benefits to emerge from a high investment in the latest IT scheme, have all served to heighten scepticism. Managers and employees now need to understand the what, why and how of change, as well as being reassured about 'What is in it for me?' before they are willing to commit themselves. Directors and senior managers may rightly feel that they know how to manage the next change, but the quid pro quo is that employees are now much more sensitive to the implications of change, and need to be inspired and persuaded. The old concept of 'resistance to change' is now being replaced by a level of sophistication and battle weariness about change which demands a true proposition about the 'value added' to all of the stakeholders in change.

The challenge to be faced is one of change leadership and not change management. All staff need to be inspired by their leader's vision, to trust them to deliver their stated intent in practice, to feel valued and important in the planning of change – these are basic, yet very personal requirements.

Our HR colleagues who contributed their cases have sought to resolve these change leadership challenges by addressing the issues of the business fit and benefit, leadership behaviour and values, and the centrality of culture change.

The business fit and benefit

The stated business and, hence, the projected benefits in change include:

- enhancing customer service and reputation
- proving that we are the first to spot and respond to market opportunities
- ensuring that customer loyalty is linked with employee loyalty
- building a world-class operation
- creating manufacturing centres of excellence
- demonstrating quality accreditation and assurance
- emphasising a strategic focus on existing business performance and future growth via innovation and diversification.

All of these business imperatives, crucial in a rapidly changing and increasingly complex market-place, were reinforced by a clear and visible change leadership philosophy that emphasised:

- the fit with the MD's and top team's vision of the future of that business
- clarity around organisation values, which all recognised the importance placed on the potential in people and the shared responsibility to deliver customer benefit, internally and externally, and also continuous change and improvement
- the need to benchmark, learn from best practice, and seek the competitive edge through people.

A common commitment throughout all the change initiatives was the importance of communicating and living a philosophy of 'making the difference through people'. An essential plank for successful change is one which publicly recognises and values the potential in people to face the need for change constructively, to be ready to learn and grow themselves, and to be innovative. This is a dramatic difference when compared with the conventional wisdom about people's inertia and resistance to change. A new paradigm appears to be emerging concerning the need for all employees to recognise and accept the requirement to respond and adapt to external change, speedily and innovatively, in ways that ensure competitive advantage, customer loyalty and future business success and, perhaps, business and personal survival.

The other key factor emerging is the importance of benchmarking, and the drive to learn from others in striving for centres of excellence and being world-class. A pragmatic focus emerges on the reality of mission and values in practice, underpinned by the concept of building a learning organisation. The emphasis is on the importance of an external, customer and competitive focus. A dramatically different orientation is articulated which emphasises the importance of adopting an external focus as against any company's belief that it can control and dominate the market-place by the quality and effectiveness of its internal processes.

Leadership behaviour and values

All of the research on effective change leadership emphasises the need for visible top leadership and commitment. Our case-studies reinforce that philosophy. The case examples emphasise the need not only to articulate corporate mission and values, but also to ensure they are fully integrated into the on-going processes of planning, reviewing and rewarding. The concept of 'values in action', and the measurables within it, are important indications of the way forward in the successful, responsive and innovative business of the future.

The centrality of culture change

All of the cases reinforce the importance of addressing and changing culture which, for all of us in the HR world, is both welcomed and challenging. The transformation agenda needing to be addressed is set out in Table 5.

The interesting lessons emerging relate to seeing culture change not as some sort of missionary and intellectual process, pursued by caring management, but more in terms of hard-nosed thinking about competitive advantage and business benefit. For HR, the key challenge in influencing change thinking is about making clear the links between the critical business success factors and the cultural change implications.

A commitment to a core programme of culture development clearly requires the following change planning considerations:

- an assessment of the pervading management style and practices
- the need to go with the traditional culture rather than against it; a 'ju-jitsu' style of intervention which uses the existing strengths, energy and focus as levers for change
- careful planning, commitment and the building of understanding
- a recognition of the investment required in the participation of the line and HR in change

Table 5 *Culture change*

Away from	Towards
● short-term, tactical thinking	● longer-term, strategic thinking
● mistrust and suspicion	● trust and shared confidence
● hierarchical management	● team-based processes and relationships
● directive, top-down management	● open communication and involvement
● Change as a top management responsibility	● partners in change
● change is interruptive	● change is endemic
● people trained to do a job	● people's capability and drive to learn continuously
● unions as negotiators of change	● unions as a constructive force
● negative assumptions about people	● openness and positive expectations
● functional thinking and internal control	● common purpose to outperform the competition
● command-and-control thinking	● all employees need to feel customer-focused, empowered and continuously learning
● people are disposable	● people can really make the difference

● planning task forces to build a critical mass and momentum for change
● an assessment at the outset of the risks in, and potential blocks to, change
● the importance of stepwise, pragmatic change and regular 'sanity checks'
● the need for sufficient well-trained facilitators who can sustain the change debate and focus.

A telling comment was that if the aim is to be world-class, then there needs to be an all-consuming and all-pervading consciousness of the need for continuous review, benchmarking, learning and adaptation.

World-class is a tough and changing standard to deliver; in HR terms it is more to do with mind sets, attitudes, quality of people, and the requirements for world-class leadership and products and services. Employees can readily recognise 'flavour of the month' headlines; they, and the successful change leaders of the future, should know that credibility has to be earned internally before projecting it externally.

The need for an integrated and well-planned influencing strategy

The clear recognition that emerges is that successful change is about realigning the balance of power, people's attitudes and perspectives, and the nature and quality of relationships. A holistic, as distinct from a remedial, perspective solution is evident. That being the case, then there is a need to consider the impact on all of the various stakeholders in change: directors, managers, supervisors, employees, unions, customers, contractors and the local community.

A thorough diagnosis of where we are now and the impact of the baggage of history and traditional thinking has emerged as the starting point for any planned cultural change strategy. If a tough-minded bottom-line management style exists, then the intervention approach has to align itself with a perceived impact on the trading success and accountability of managers. In this, equating change success with bottom-line contribution can serve to enhance the credibility of HR as an effective influencer.

Much care and attention runs through all the cases to align the planned HR intervention with the existing perceived value set. The avoidance of the risks involved in a too confrontational and challenging approach is all too evident.

In the diagnosis of the current situation, key factors are:

- the existing and traditional leadership style and approach
- the way managers are judged and held accountable, and rewarded
- the time horizon and perspectives of thinking from the tactical, reactive through to the strategic, proactive
- the attitudes to risk-taking
- the vested interests of the various power players and groups; the identification of the levers for change and the pressures to maintain the *status quo*
- the attitudes to people, from the autocratic to the developmental
- the track record in change and the consequences in terms of employee attitudes and readiness to embrace further change
- the impact of existing policies, procedures and practices, eg, if an innovative culture is required, is that in line with the managerial competencies valued and promoted, or is conformity sought?
- the choice of strategy from the revolutionary to the evolutionary; the apparent preference is towards the pragmatic and practical, rather than the radical.

It is also interesting to note that, whether the diagnosis is thorough and deliberate or intuitive, the influencing approach emerging ranges from the behind-the-scenes coaching and counselling of directors and managers through to a heavily rational approach based on extensive task force structure making the logical case for change. The concept of direct and planned HR/ organisation development interventions where a public challenge to the organisation is made appears to be avoided.

A perceived value-set in terms of influencing approach is either empowerment through coaching and/or major change through study groups and analysis. Patience, pragmatism, sanity and caution are words which seem to ring in the minds of the HR people involved. Influence appears to be concerned with seeding ideas and testing the boundaries; educating and empowering managers; demonstrating the rationale for change through task forces; benchmarking to seek competitive advantage. This orientation positions the pace-setters in change as the line directors and managers, with HR in a facilitating role.

Other insights emerge concerning the power of new blood. The proposition emerging appears to be one of 'fresh minds', 'seeing the wood for the trees', and the price of indoctrination in the old habits and policies. This is an implicit comment on the consequences of the previous management development regime.

On the choice of influencing approach, the model shown in Figure 19 appears to be pertinent.

Figure 19
Choice of influencing style

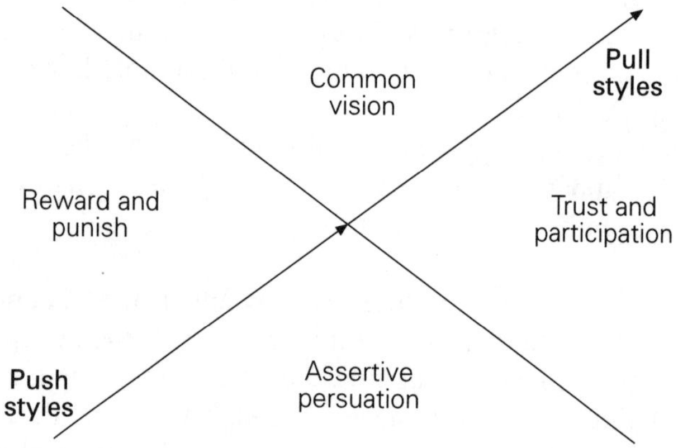

In this model 'push styles of influence' are through:

- the use of reward and judgement system; a 'carrot and stick' approach (the reward and punish style)
- the impact of one's own personality and track record; a follow-me style 'because I have been there and done it and I have the power and authority to make it happen' (the assertive persuasion style)

The 'pull styles' are through:

- a shared diagnosis of the need for change, coupled with a common vision of the way forward; an emphasis on shaping the future together and rational analysis, research and planning (the common vision style)
- a high investment of time in building mutual trust and respect, leading to an assessment that 'we together can change the world because we believe in and value the same things, and whatever happens we will support each other' (the trust and participation style).

The emerging influencing logic is the need to have people who:

- support the need for change through benchmarking, analysis and research
- are inspired by a vision of competitive advantage through valuing people
- feel in charge of the pace and depth of change through pragmatism and carefully paced consideration
- see the benefits from learned experience and recognise that change will be planned and evolutionary, rather than radical and revolutionary.

In this way the risks in change appear to be manageable and the benefits deliverable.

Our case-studies appear to reinforce the need for 'pull styles' of influence, as distinct from the 'push styles' with their emphasis on personal and organisational power. For HR, the core change leadership competencies appear to be in building a common vision and developing mutual trust and participation. The emphasis on joint line/HR development of the change propositions, together with the coaching and mentoring approach, illustrates this philosophy. Table 6 outlines a model that is common to many of the case-studies. This indicates a cautious, planned, thorough philosophy based on stepwise learning and adaptation.

Table 6 *A strategy for change*

A	+B	+C	+D	>Z
The shared and owned acceptance of the need for change	Building a common vision of the future	Planning and taking pragmatic steps forward	Demonstrating the benefits in change at the business and people levels	Showing that the risks in avoiding change are high

Positioning HR as a strategic change partner

In our previous IPD Book, *Empowering Change: The role of people management*, we emphasised the need for HR to position itself as a strategic partner in change as distinct from the custodian of HR policies and practices. The case-studies clearly demonstrate support for this shift in HR influence.

A whole array of examples emerges showing how the HR professionals involved have sought to demonstrate the credibility and value of HR in this strategic partner role. The spectrum of interventions here is in itself educative for the HR professional who wishes to be not only heard but also influential at the top team table.

HR as a strategic partner

Practical steps:

- joint HR/line formulation of HR strategy which is driven by the business strategy and competitiveness sought
- transfer of HR responsibilities to the line to free HR to act in a change facilitation/counselling role
- co-coaching and facilitation of top team colleagues' responses to the demands of the change leadership role
- demonstrating the bottom-line benefit to trading performance through behind-the-scenes mentoring

- surveying and demonstrating the impact of employee morale on employee loyalty and pride, and the knock-on influence on customer service and loyalty
- carrying out surveys on the impact of the HR role and hence acting as a role model for a customer-service orientation with a readiness to seek feedback and challenge
- becoming the challenging conscience for the organisation in terms of the stated mission, values and intended behaviour
- introducing upward appraisal, customer feedback and 360° challenge processes
- acting as the champion for empowerment throughout the organisation by adopting a coaching and mentoring style
- proving the readiness of people to want to learn and grow and, hence, assuaging normal fears about overcoming resistance to change.

The concerns expressed are about shaking off the traditional image and reputation of HR and striving to demonstrate a new added value. For HR the drive appears to be to take on the role and skills of the internal OD/change consultant. The dilemmas faced are not *'should HR change its role and influence?'* a case which is well made, but *'how do we set about doing this?'* The keys are in the hearts and minds of the HR professionals. All thinking HR people are well aware of the importance of the people dimensions in change; the core dilemma is about whether they have the courage to challenge themselves and not allow, perhaps, their own personal career survival agenda to subordinate the needs of other people. Future business success will, in substantial part, be determined by the behaviour of the HR function as champions of people's needs and fears in change.

Agreeing a change leadership style and approach

Our case providers also demonstrate a high willingness to learn and adapt themselves. Their search for new self-understanding and awareness appears in many cases to be the catalyst for a new leadership and management attitude. The enthusiasm generated by HR in the search for new boundaries and insights appears to rub off on the line managers involved. Change requires vision, passion and enthusiasm; for HR the challenge thrown down is to demonstrate this.

Clear examples also emerge of top teams being ready to 'hold the mirror up' to themselves and seek to change their leadership impact and behaviour. A high level of leadership responsibility and maturity is portrayed. In essence, a stance is taken of being willing to 'stand up and be counted', which demonstrates a willingness to become a leadership role model to the rest of the organisation.

The interesting insights are that these review processes aim to reposition the top team's role as change visionaries, strategists and leaders. For them, the biggest problem is letting go of day-to-day control and devolving responsibility to proven and capable senior and middle management. The leadership preference for financial, operational detail and hands-on command-and-control still appears to persist. The HR role positioning of coach, mentor and counsellor demonstrates the levels of top leadership concerns and fears.

Programmes of self-awareness, personal stocktaking and knowledge are apparent. The concept of director-level personal development appears to be at the core of the change leadership agenda, and a healthy attitude to personal learning emerges.

In terms of change leadership approach, the choices demonstrated appear to be:

- 'middle up and out' change: where middle and senior management are empowered through training, task forces, surveys and consultation to make the case for change
- an emphasis on customer service-chain performance review and improvement, where the concepts of customer focus – both internally and externally – are dominant
- a focus on flexible working practices, self-managed teams positioned as the key to new shop floor practices, all aimed at enhancing productivity and full line utilisation.

- 'values in action' programmes, where a challenge process is cascaded into the organisation as a driver for stocktaking and improvement planning, to secure competitive advantage through living the business values in practice.

This focus shows that the lessons of history in terms of open-ended culture change programmes for their own sake appear to have been well learned. For HR, the challenge as a strategic partner is to work with the line to demonstrate the business benefits sought through people. The most telling change concept is the introduction of an HR philosophy which aims to ensure that 'people really make the difference'; a set of beliefs which recognises that it is people, together, who can solve problems, respond innovatively to new challenges, rather than systems and organisational processes.

Confronting oneself as a change agent and influencer

Throughout the chapters in Part I we sought to provide you with frameworks for personal stocktaking and self-development. It is interesting to note how our HR colleagues who have presented their case-studies have resolved their own internal dilemmas. For them the personal beliefs and values emerging are evident, embracing:

- the potential in people to learn and adapt
- the empowerment of people to move from a reactive, defensive posture to change towards becoming proactive, confident influencers
- the importance of collaboration and teamworking and the avoidance of confrontation and potential conflict
- the need for the line and top management to be and be seen as change leaders
- the care required to judge the pace and depth of change and test the acceptable boundaries

- the need to match and build on the business needs and values, rather than confront them directly.

The choices made demonstrate a tendency to lean towards the coaching and counselling styles, the educational approach to learning from benchmarking and research, and rational and logical case development through extensive consultation and participation. The direct interventionist approach seems to be limited to one-to-one and small team workshops. The power of the survey and of feedback is also evident.

If HR is to become a credible, influential strategic partner, we believe that many of the skills, techniques and strategies of the organisation development and effectiveness consultant will be required. Without these, HR people who wish to be perceived as effective change influencers could be constraining themselves and their impact by their own fear of failure, risk aversion, and tendency to rely on rational argument and persuasion, without exploring their own personal comfort zones. The innovative, adaptive organisation of the future may require higher levels of intuition, sharing of feelings and confronting the 'here and now' and blocks to creativity and self-realisation.

Our case-studies illustrate the potency of building partnerships in change. A new psychological contract and partnership between HR and the business may well be required. For HR people, to be impactful today and tomorrow, it could well be that they need a heightened level of self-awareness, knowledge, mentoring and coaching. A dose of the medicine of practising what we preach may well be needed.

Our case-study presenters have clearly found participating in the journey of change personally rewarding, empowering and highly developmental. Having tasted these fruits of learning, the readiness and appetite for the next change challenge is demonstrably there. For HR as a function, this process needs to be nurtured and developed. Without this, HR could be condemned to the role of the reactive policy writer and custodian. A lose/ lose scenario for people and organisations could easily emerge.

Developing the HR function as a credible change influencer and partner

If you wish to commit your HR function to becoming a credible and influential change partner, then our case-studies highlight the interventions possible. In Tables 7 to 9 we re-emphasise our model of change leadership competencies.

The information in Tables 7 to 9 serves to demonstrate that in the influential HR function of the future there will be a need to build up a kit-bag of potential interventions. This should be paralleled by a consciousness on the part of the HR community continually to challenge current thinking and practices and strive for the next breakthrough and business transformation insight. To be too busy on today's issues can put at risk tomorrow's solutions.

Table 7 *HR as a change visionary*

	Practical interventions
Shaping competencies	● business mission and values linked to culture change ● business strategy and HR strategy ● competitive advantage through people ● business critical success factors and culture ● co-operative partnerships on future change ● innovative/responsive organisations.
Scanning and interrogating competencies	● organisation of the future ● risk assessment (customer service and loyalty/market change/ technological trends) ● benchmarking ● globalisation ● diagnosis of organisation health and responsiveness.

Table 8 *HR as a change influencer*

	Practical interventions
Standing apart competencies	• employee surveys • customer surveys • benchmarking • 360° appraisal • management development strategy reviews • culture audits • values in practice • leadership impact feedback
Organisation-influencing competencies	• task force structures • mentoring/coaching • empowerment/self-development • HR as a change champion/ strategic partner • business strategy/competitive advantage through people/ culture change • mission and value exercises

Table 9 *HR as a change facilitator*

	Practical interventions
Open-minded competencies	• mission and values exercises which test current practices • devolution/empowerment initiatives • trust/relationship-building • business/HR strategy planning conferences • middle-up feedback processes
Empathising/empowering competencies	• change leadership workshops • HR as strategic partner skills development • MD/director counselling • interpersonal skills training • self-awareness/development programmes • influencing skills training • the learning organisation
Innovation competencies	• task forces • critical business processes reviews • blocks to creativity workshops • managing for continuous improvement workshops

Part III

Change Leadership in the Organisation of the Future:
The Challenge to HR

15

Where HR is now

The following might be considered an apt comment on the views of other managers on the HR manager:

> When Aeschines spoke, they said 'How well he speaks', but when Demosthenes spoke they said, 'Let us march against Philip.'

The HR manager seems to be regarded as Aeschines, others generally feel they are articulate, and have a high oral communication competency. However, they are not generally considered to be the manager that others will follow – they are not Demosthenes.

The basis for this assertion is the results of a survey carried out by Hugh Gibbons of PsyPHAA and an additional survey undertaken by ODL. A mailshot questionnaire was sent to 117 managers. Their responses are shown in Table 10. Managers were asked: 'In your experience, which directors lead major changes?'

Table 10

	A lot				A little
	1	**2**	**3**	**4**	**5**
General managers	✔				
Finance directors			✔		
Marketing directors		✔			
R&D directors			✔		
Sales directors			✔		
HR directors				✔	

It is interesting to observe that the HR director is considered to be the senior manager who is least likely to lead change.

The issues raised by this question are, 'What is it about HR directors that makes others judge that they are unlikely to lead change in comparison with other professionals?'; 'What do HR directors lack that finance, marketing, R&D and sales directors have?' Those questions were put by telephone to 20 senior managers – in finance, sales, marketing and R&D. Their responses can be summarised as follows. HR directors, it was felt,

- do not have the business experience to lead change
- are not assertive enough
- might be innovative but they rarely exhibit their ideas rapidly enough
- do not understand business, therefore they can't lead change in it
- are facilitators; they do not push us to change, rather they help us manage the change we direct
- have no charisma
- do not have the capacity to envision overall business changes
- would be in marketing if they wanted to lead change
- are too cautious to lead change.

It would seem that HR directors have a considerable need to develop their image if they are to be perceived as change leaders or strategic partners in change.

A second survey question was asked: 'In your experience, how do different directors rate on their change skills?' Table 11 shows the mean responses of 167 managers.

The survey seems to show that HR directors are perceived as researchers and facilitators, but not influencers.

The telephone interviewees were asked, 'What is it about sales, marketing and general managers that makes them more able to influence change than HR directors?' Their responses can be summarised as follows. HR directors, it was felt,

- are not tough
- are reactive, whereas marketing, sales and general managers are proactive
- are too risk-averse
- do not act until they ask marketing, sales, general manager or others for their opinions, whereas other directors act on their own
- do not insist on their view – they wait for others and support them
- tend not to be confident and independent, whereas marketing, sales and general managers are
- are too ready to adapt to others' views; marketing, sales, and general managers tend to be firm about theirs.

The HR director thus has an image problem.

Table 11

	Change researcher	Change influencer	Change facilitator
General managers	3.8	4.2	2.8
Finance directors	2.6	2.5	2.0
Marketing directors	4.2	4.0	2.9
R&D directors	3.2	2.5	2.1
Sales directors	2.5	3.4	2.7
HR directors	3.4	2.7	3.5

Key   Change facilitator   = Helpers/counsellors
        Change researcher   = Recognisers of strategic vision
        Change influencer   = Positive, assertive pushers of others

Ratings   1 = least skilled
            2 = below average skill
            3 = average skill
            4 = above average skill
            5 = most skilled

By developing their change leader skills, it would be expected
that a similar survey in a few years' time would exhibit a
different set of responses. If HR Directors could be rated 4.0 and
above as visionary and influencer, while retaining or increasing
the rating as facilitator, they may be rated as the director who
would lead major change.

16

■ Equipping Yourself for the Future

We hope that our comments, your self-exploration, and the experiences of other HR change leaders, have enriched your understanding of yourself and your development opportunities. However, we recognise that, although our journey was through 15 chapters, yours is still continuing. Some thoughts of others on travel might therefore be helpful:

> Every perfect traveller always creates the country where he travels.
>
> Nikos Kazantzakis

> The traveller's eye-view of men and women is not satisfying. A man might spend his life in trains and restaurants and know nothing of humanity at the end. To know, one must be an actor as well as a spectator.
>
> Aldous Huxley

Our central thrust has been a stress on leadership. Many current organisational analysts seem to have devalued the role of the leader. There almost seems to be the assumption that the organisational landscape: structure, roles, processes, practices and procedures, will totally determine the actions of the organisation's members. Our thesis has been the reverse. We have posited that the leader is the major determinant of organisational success.

We have discovered that managers who are successful leaders will be those who have a higher level of thinking power, who can, more than others, rapidly assimilate and analyse information and from this can create an organisational vision. The vision probably contains a considerable element of innovation. Additionally, the leaders are able to persuade others that their vision should be adopted and will be able to excite and commit others to that vision. Their competence will include a wide range of influence skills, so that they will be capable of convincing others from a range of cultures, functions, positions and levels of authority. Finally, they will be capable of ensuring that those who are affected by the changes are facilitated – thus ensuring that they do not suffer debilitating stress and that they are developed to ensure they have the competencies required for the changed organisational situation.

These are demanding goals, and we have therefore set out a few suggestions about development routes to maximise your potential as a change leader. Most obviously, you should seek information wherever you can about significant industrial, economic and social trends which are likely to impinge on your business. Effective action has always involved risk, and the future is now more dynamic and uncertain than ever before; but although you need to be cautious about the speculations of forecasters and futurologists, there is no excuse for ignoring them.

Another key issue is personal resilience. If you hope not only to withstand the pressures of rapid change but to gain positive enjoyment from the experience, you will need to acquire a repertoire of stress-coping skills. The following list is far from exhaustive, but it should none the less prove useful:

- meditation
- relaxation tapes
  - muscular, where you gradually relax each muscle
  - breathing, where you gradually slow down your breathing rate
  - auditory, where you listen to some Gregorian chant or the sound of the sea.
- visualisation
  - where, in a relaxed state, you visualise some scene that makes you feel good.
- physical exercise
- diet
  - take extra Vitamin 'B' (this is depleted by stress)
  - reduce coffee intake (caffeine increases heart rate)

- reduce alcohol intake to about three units per day
- reduce saturated fat intake (it is increased during stress)
- drugs: for some stress-related conditions these are a temporary aid. Long-term stress-coping needs a personal, rather than a pharmacological, solution.
- seek a facilitator to help you cope. Counselling might help you to understand yourself and the causes of your stress and thereby help you identify how to cope more effectively.

The future change leader will need to be more open to:

- him- or herself
- others
- culture
- ideas.

To develop this increased openness, HR managers should seek experience outside their:

- function
- organisation
- culture
- philosophy
- education.

We would even like to make a final provocative suggestion that the HR change leader of the future will be someone whose:

- reading includes French philosophy and Chinese theology
- conferences include cosmology
- personal education includes the maths of chaos theory
- interests include the ecology of Borneo.

If this sounds like the menu for a polymath, then perhaps that is what the future change leader will need to be. Like Huxley, they will need to view their visions as potentially revolutionary.

> Every great advance in national knowledge has involved the absolute rejection of authority.

or

> Sit down before a fact as a little child; be prepared to give up every preconceived notion, follow humbly wherever and whatever abyss nature leads, or you shall learn nothing.

Knowing the simple rule or equation that governs a system is not always sufficient to predict its behaviour. And, conversely, exceedingly complicated patterns of behaviour may derive not from exceedingly complex causes, but from the chaotic workings of some very simple algorith. Anyone interested in pursuing this theme should look at one of the many excellent recent introductions to chaos theory.

A final thought:

The Autolycus syndrome

In Shakespeare's *The Winter's Tale* Autolycus is described as a 'snapper-up of unconsidered trifles'. Using this concept in management would be to explore how some managers spot 'trifles' while others do not; of these, how some seize them and how even fewer find a novel use for them. Like clothes left drying on a hedge or washing line, many ideas are unprotected and deserve to be snatched.

Leaders who identify the 'trifles' will be those who, in an ambiguous environment, have the capability to spot differences, to determine the patterns in unconnected data, and thus to perceive the factors that are relevant.

Seizing the 'trifles' requires that the leader has not only the vision to recognise the potential but has the proactivity, assertiveness, risk-taking ability and speed of response to snatch them from the hedge before others act. Leaders who seize the idea will be those who have influence. They have to identify the idea, capture it and use it before the person who has it recognises its value and ensures that it is protected. They take the risk because they may be 'caught'.

Autolycus was a thief and therefore a marginal man. Those who have the Autolycus syndrome are also marginal. They spot ideas that others do not and then they make public the ideas that others might not understand or appreciate.

In a chaotic environment it is likely that the major breakthroughs will occur through an almost random interconnection of ideas. Thus, although a leader may be able to spot, seize and make public an idea, the maximum opportunity for a breakthrough will usually occur when that leader is also a facilitator who has created an organisational climate where 'upward and lateral challenge is encouraged, risk is rewarded and where failure is learned from, not punished'. Autolycus can, in this atmosphere, not only seize his idea but have the opportunity to seize others, interconnect them and have them altered and amended by others.

In chaotic times, therefore, the Autolycus syndrome is a major part of the profile of the strategic change leader. The 'trifle' may need to be put into a strategic context, but still the core idea is vital – just as the oyster without grit will not produce a pearl.

> In chaos, the marginal man is the compass and map to the breakthrough.
>
> C C Ridgeway

 **Appendix**

TSB Linking Business and HR Strategies: 'Making the Difference through People'

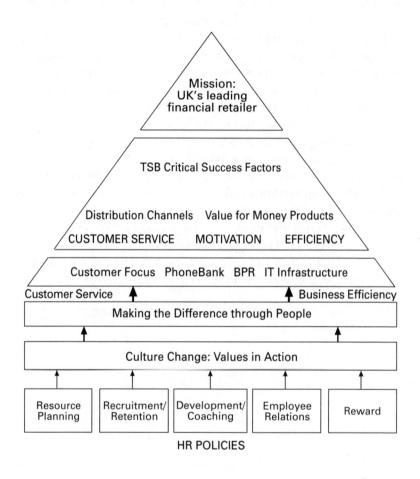

■ References

DE VRIES K. M. (1991) *Organisations on the Couch*. San Francisco, Jossey-Bass.

DE VRIES K.M. (1995) *Organisational Paradoxes*. London, Routledge.

EGAN G. (1975) *The Skilled Helper*. California, Wadsworth Publishing.

FOMBRUN C. AND TICHY N. (1984) 'Strategic planning and human resource management', in Lamb (ed.), *Competitive Strategic Management*, Englewood Cliffs, Prentice Hall, 312–32.

FREUD S. (1904) *Three Essays on the History of Sexuality*. Standard Edition 7. London, Hogarth Press.

FREUD S. (1921) *Group Psychology and the Analysis of the Ego*. Standard Edition 12. London, Hogarth Press.

STOREY J. (1989) *New Perspectives on Human Resource Management*. London, Routledge.

STOREY J. (1992) *Developments in the Management of Human Resources*. Oxford, Blackwell.

Index